CONTENTS

❖

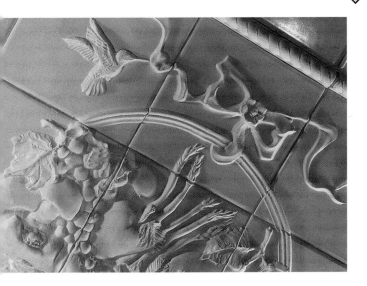

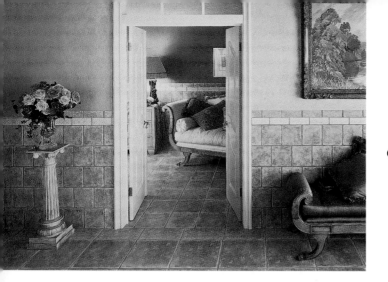

Tiling

The Installation Handbook

Edward R. Lipinski

STERLING PUBLISHING CO., INC.
NEW YORK

Library of Congress Cataloging-in-Publication Data

Lipinski, Edward R., 1943-

      Tiling: the installation handbook/Edward R. Lipinski.

         p. cm.

      Includes index.

      ISBN 0-8069-6115-5

         1. Tile laying--Amateurs' manuals. 2. Flooring, Tile--Amateurs' manuals. 3. Dwellings, Remodeling--Amateurs' manuals. 4. Walls--Amateurs' manuals. 5. Tiles in interior decoration--Amateurs' manuals. I. Title.

TH8531 .L57 2002

698--dc21   2002066871

10 9 8 7 6 5 4 3 2 1

Published by Sterling Publishing Co., Inc.

387 Park Avenue South, New York, N.Y. 10016

© 2002 by Edward R. Lipinski

Distributed in Canada by Sterling Publishing

c/o Canadian Manda Group, One Atlantic Avenue, Suite 105

Toronto, Ontario, Canada M6K 3E7

Distributed in Great Britain and Europe by Chyrysalis Books

64 Brewery Road, London N7 9NT, England

Distributed in Australia by Capricorn Link (Australia) Pty Ltd.

P.O. Box 704, Windsor, NSW 2756, Australia

Printed in China

All rights reserved

Sterling ISBN 0-8069-6115-5

DESIGN BY RENATO STANISIC

INTRODUCTION

I have been writing and illustrating how-to articles and books for over two decades now. I have also been involved in various aspects of residential construction, so I have firsthand knowledge of many of the techniques of building and remodeling.

I approached this project as I do all my articles. Rather than simply relying on my own experience, I talked to professionals in the field and read other information so that I could be aware of the latest methods and materials available to the do-it-yourselfer. I had assumed that the topic of tile installation would be fairly straightforward. After all, the crafts of tile-making and installation have been around for over 8,000 years. *(See Chapter 1.)*

I was rather surprised to find out how much difference of opinion there is among tile setters as to the best materials to use and the ideal methods for using them. While everyone is entitled to his opinion, I believe that there are two fundamental reasons for these differing points of view.

Some tile setters set a high priority on permanence. They want the finished job to stand the test of time and will, therefore, go to great lengths to ensure that the installation will withstand all foreseeable wear, tear, and environmental forces. Consequently, they use the thickest substrates, install waterproof membranes wherever and whenever possible, and use expansion joints around all joints

Even a fairly complicated installation such as this one is possible with the proper knowledge and planning.
(Photo courtesy of Crossville Porcelain Stone / USA)

and perimeters. For them, there can be no compromise with the quality of materials or methods.

As laudable as these goals are, other tile setters point out they can be expensive and are often impractical. Everyone wants a tile installation to be durable and relatively maintenance-free; but most people acknowledge that sooner or later the remodeling bug will bite. When this happens, the installation, no matter how beautiful, will have to go to make room for something more contemporary. The goal, then, is to install the best possible job that will stand for the immediate future without going overboard on those costly items that are only needed for ultra-permanent situations.

Admittedly both schools of thought have their merits, and it is difficult to totally ignore one in favor of the other. So it seems that tile setting, like life, requires some compromises. In writing this book, then, I have tried to present both sides of debatable issues and to cover the advantages and disadvantages of the wide variety of materials available and methods used. In this way, the reader can understand the problems involved, evaluate the benefits of the available choices, and then judge for himself the best course of action. Even if the reader does not intend to do his own tile installation, he will still be equipped to discuss any plans or projects with professionals and voice his preferences or at least understand the methods employed by the workers.

Tile pattern can be achieved in two ways. One way is to install tiles made with patterns in their texture or in their color. Another way is to alternate the arrangement of the tiles or to use tiles of different shapes and varying colors.

1

Tile History

Archaeologists and industrial historians can only conjecture on how tile manufacture began and evolved into an industry. It seems it was born out of necessity. Lacking a plentiful supply of wood and unable to work stone with primitive hand tools, prehistoric builders undoubtedly mined the soft clay soil on the riverbanks and shaped it into bricks. They hardened the bricks by allowing them to dry in the sun.

At some point, someone must have noticed that the bricks used around ovens or fireplaces were harder and more durable than those left in the sun to dry. Obviously, the intense heat of the fire gave the surrounding bricks a hardness that sun drying could not. It only remained, then, to build special fireplaces to fire the mud bricks and impart that durability to them. It's most likely that the first kilns were simply open pits with a central fire. Later, sometime before 3,000 B.C., brick makers found that enclosed ovens

1–1 (opposite page). *The face of this fireplace is tiled with Flemish-styled tiles. These blue and white tile motifs originated with craftsmen in Flanders during the Middle Ages and Renaissance, who used them to add a decorative touch. These traditional designs are still available in contemporary products, and are particularly desirable as decorative accents in period-style homes. As a complement to this design, the hearth is paved with tiles featuring a rustic glaze and texture.* **(Photo courtesy of Lis King Tile Company)** allowed greater control over the firing process.

No one can say exactly where or when tile manufacture developed. It's most likely that it started in the Middle East around Mesopotamia or in Ancient Egypt. It was in these regions that the first great civilizations of antiquity were born.

Bits of tile that date back 12,000 to 18,000 years have been found by archaeologists along the Nile River. Ancient Egypt has been called the cradle of the glassmaking industry, so it is natural that the first colored glazes would be produced there. These were copper glazes produced in the fourth millennium B.C. The glazing was not used extensively on large areas of tile. Instead it seems to have been used mainly for inlaying and producing small sections with different colors encrusted on the surface.

The ancient Egyptians seem to have had a preference for blue faience,[1] possibly because it had a religious significance, and it was used on tombstones as well as for tile decoration. Egyptian glazes[2] were more transparent than those used in Asia Minor. Still the Egyptians managed to achieve intricate and subtle effects by applying the glaze in layers and by incising decorations into the tiles before glazing. The glaze would fill into these cuts and depressions in greater depth than on the surrounding surface. The final effect was that the design appeared in deeper color than that of the background.

Archeological evidence shows that mud brick manufacture was carried on in Ali Kosh, Iran as early as 7,500 B.C. Tile-making began later. Tiles decorated with white- and blue-striped patterns dating back to 4,000 B.C. were produced in El Ubaid or Samarra. Unlike Egypt, Mesopotamia experienced considerable political turmoil and was often a battleground between advancing cultures. In the seventh century B.C., Babylon experienced a flourishing renaissance under the Chaldean king, Nebuchadnezzar II. During this time, impressive ziggurats[3] (the biblical Tower of Babel and the temple of Marduk) were constructed, as well as the famous gates of Ishtar.

These edifices were built with mud brick. Later, glazed tiles were used to decorate entire walls. The colors used in these tiles were chosen for their religious or political significance. City walls were yellow, gates blue, temples white, and the palaces bright red. Decorations and images made of glazed tiles were also integrated into the surfaces.

The gates of Ishtar (1-2), for example, had a relief of lions 10 feet (three meters) high in brilliant colors on either side of the entrance. These images served as more than decoration, and were intended, no doubt, to instill fear and awe in the heart of any visitor and perhaps to serve as a warning that he should not enter the temples unless his heart was pure.

Other images on the gates and surrounding walls include figures representing the bodyguard of the Achaemenid princes and a curious dragon-like creature often called the Musrussu dragon. The dragon is rendered in ocher and brown tones and appears on a field of blue tiles. It has the forefeet of a lion, the

---

1. Faience is earthenware decorated with opaque-colored glazes. **2.** A glaze is a mixture, usually transparent or translucent, that's applied to the surface of ceramic wares and, when heated, forms a moisture-impervious coating. **3.** Ziggurats are Mesopotamian temple towers consisting of a pyramidal structure built in successive stages with outside spiraling staircases and a shrine at top.

back feet of an eagle, the body of a bull, and the head of a serpent. In all, the outer gate of the Ishtar complex had over 10,000 glazed tiles covering its surface.

The Greeks and Romans used tiles in the form of mosaics to decorate the interiors of temples and public buildings. From the first century B.C., the Romans used mosaic tile as an important decorative or functional element in all buildings, both public and private. Some of these served as practical coverings for kitchens and baths, while others depicted historical or mythological scenes in large rooms of public buildings or private houses. They also used decorative tiles as roof ornaments. These pieces were of semicircular shape with relief ornamentation.

It should be pointed out, however, that the mosaics and tiles were seen as a decorative addition to the architecture, similar to our practice of hanging pictures on a wall. In the Greco-Roman world, designers and builders preferred to let the interplay of thrust and support generated by supports and beams of the architectural elements define a structure. Concrete and carved stone replaced brick and tile. This remained the norm in Western architecture up to, and including, contemporary times.

In the East, tile-making continued to be an important art form. Fine white stoneware along with architectural and tomb tiles were produced during the Shang-Yin dynasty and later in the Han dynasty.

In the Middle East, however, tile and indeed most art forms entered a state of dormancy when the civilizations in that area fell

1–2. *Glazed tiles from the Ishtar Gate built by Nebuchadnezzar.* **(Metropolitan Museum of Art)**

under the yoke of Greek, and then, Roman masters. With the fall of the Roman Empire and the rise of Islam, the Middle East experienced a cultural rebirth. Arts and sciences flourished and tile-making reached a level in manufacture and design that has never been surpassed even to this day.

The palace in Samarra, constructed between A.D. 835 and 880, had walls decorated with glazed tiles. Many of the designs on the tiles, a cockerel surrounded by a wreath, for example, seem to have been inspired by Sassanian textile designs.[4] Another source of inspiration and stimulation for tile-making and pottery design came from increased trade with China.

Tile and pottery manufacture was largely concentrated in one area at a time. These manufacturing sites shifted with the tides of political and economic fortune. Baghdad was

---

4. The Sassanian dynasties were established in A.D. 224 by Ardeshir, a descendant of Sassan (an early Persian king). Ardeshir and later his son, Shapus, created a vast empire that remained until the seventh century.

1–3. *Fourteenth-century star-shaped tiles in Iran—Chinese influence.* **(Metropolitan Museum of Art)**

the important center in the ninth century, but when the glory of the caliphates[5] waned, tile-making gradually shifted to Egypt. After Saladin's[6] victory over the Fatimids,[7] tile manufacture moved to northern Mesopotamia and then Persia. Tile-making was so highly prized as an art form that conquering armies would often abduct the tile makers as part of the spoils of war.

These migrations resulted in styles and techniques that absorbed a broad spectrum of regional influences and tastes and make it difficult to distinguish between tiles made in different localities. Nevertheless, sometimes ceramic wares became so distinctive that they took the name of the places where they were produced or marketed. Thus, faience was named after Faenza (Italy), majolica after Majorca (Spain), and delft from the town of Delft (Holland).

In the town of Kashan (in present-day Iran), tile makers created tiles with brilliant reliefs, subtle delineation, and an extensive vocabulary of decorative motifs and patterns. Called *kashi* or *kashani*, the tiles have a brown luster over decorations in relief. They were used in combination with cruciform and star-shaped tiles that were painted with intricate designs. In addition to facing walls, these tiles were used in prayer niches, or *mihrabs*, in mosques.

Another style produced by the tile makers of Kashan, and perhaps also from Ravi, was the *minai* tile. These were polychromatic pieces with delicate designs, similar to illuminated manuscripts. Enamel colors fixed by a second firing[8] were used to create the wide range of colors. These tiles were produced as early as A.D. 1200.

Almost all the manufacturing and most decorating techniques used in the Middle East, and eventually in Europe and the New World, were developed in Persia. Persian decorative tiles that were bonded together to form elaborate continuous decoration or Kufic[9] inscriptions were, in fact, the forerunners of the Spanish *alicatatodos* panels of tile mosaic. These intricate wall mosaics seem to have started out as simple geometric designs, but were later expanded to include undulating, flowing lines and stylized plant forms. One outstanding use of this technique is in the celebrated Blue Mosque of Tabriz, completed in 1465.

A technique that gradually eclipsed that of tile-mosaics was cuerda seca. The term

5. The caliphs were the successors of Muhammad as temporal and spiritual heads of Islam. **6.** Saladin (1138–93) was the Muslim leader who recaptured Jerusalem from the Crusaders. **7.** The Fatimids were an Islamic dynasty that ruled Tunisia from 909 to 1051 and in Egypt from 969 to 1171. The dynasty was named after the prophet Mohammed's daughter, Fatima. **8.** A first firing hardens the tile. The glaze is then applied and fixed with another, second, firing. **9.** Kufic script was a form of early Arabic in use in the seventh century.

"cuerda seca" is Spanish, but the style and manufacture of these tiles originated in Persia. Unlike the tile-mosaic technique, which uses combinations of individual tiles in contrasting colors to form patterns, the cuerda seca technique uses tiles that are each painted with complex and intricate patterns to cover large areas in palace walls and garden pavilions.

In addition to paints and glazes, Persian craftsmen also experimented with creating tiles with textures and raised motifs. Relief work gained in popularity, because the dazzling light of the harsh sun created an interesting interplay of light and shadow across the planes of a building.

Tile-making in India utilized the same basic techniques as in Persia, probably because trade between the two countries was common and India absorbed many of the skills and styles of Persian craftsmen. Indian kings also adopted the Persian custom of decorating the walls of entrance gates with fearsome animals so that approaching visitors would be reminded of the power and sovereignty of the king. A fine example of this exists on the walls of the main gate to Lahore Fort in Northern India; a mural on the wall composed entirely of glazed tiles depicts two bull elephants locked in mortal combat.

Even though tile-making did not achieve the prominence in Europe that it enjoyed in the Middle East, it was not ignored. During the Middle Ages, tiles were used primarily as a decorative surfacing material for floors in churches and castles. The English developed a technique for inlaying tiles. A design was first pressed into the tile clay; then the impression was filled with a light-colored pipe clay. The tiles were fired, then glazed with a transparent or semi-translucent glaze, and then fired again. The finished tile had a yellow or beige design on a dark background. These patterned tiles were set in a field with plain and solid-colored tiles to create a decorated floor that resembled an oriental carpet.

Two other popular techniques used extensively during the Middle Ages were *sgraffito* and *sgrafittato*. Sgraffito tiles were made by coating a dark tile with a topcoat of light-colored clay. The design was then etched in the topcoat so the contrasting body color showed through. The result was a light-colored tile with a dark design. The sgrafittato technique was similar in that it used a dark tile with a light topcoat, but with the sgrafittato technique, the designer scraped away the background so the final design appeared as a light pattern on a dark background. By the thirteenth century, tile makers in England were also producing relief tiles in addition to the inlayed and sgraffito and sgrafittato pieces.

1–4. *Ottoman 16th-century tiles.* **(Metropolitan Museum of Art)**

Ceramic tiles were rarely used in private homes, with one notable exception: around the fireplace. Since most houses were made of wood, the central fire posed a definite hazard. This was not a community concern when homes were isolated in the country, but as towns and cities grew, any fire in the home could quickly spread and threaten the entire settlement. Therefore, communities set up ordinances requiring home owners to face their fireplaces with fireproof brick or tile. The use of fireplace tiles started in Flanders, but soon spread to other parts of Europe.

Most of these tiles were rather pedestrian with little or no decoration. Some tile makers offered tiles with low reliefs, but their design vocabulary was rather limited and lacking in variety. This is rather curious considering the fact that the fireplace was the focal point of the average home and decorative tiles would have offered a cheery contrast to the rest of the surroundings.

For the most part then, tiles were manufactured primarily for churches, temples, and palaces and for the homes of the very wealthy. They were too expensive for the average home owner, but by the nineteenth century the industrial revolution took hold and most trades were transformed from small shops into large factories. Tile-making became an industry. Ceramic tiles could now be produced in quantity at an affordable price.

Yet manufacturers offered only a limited variety of tile sizes, shapes, and colors, and most home builders thought of ceramic tile as a functional material that should be used in rooms where sanitation and cleanliness were paramount considerations. Few people, it seems, considered ceramic tile for its decorative potential. Hence tiles—most square, white pieces—were used in bathrooms and kitchens and rarely found applications in other rooms.

After World War II, the situation changed dramatically, perhaps because international travel and trade made people aware of the ways other cultures used tiles to great effect in decorating their surroundings. Tile makers began producing tiles in a wide variety of shapes, colors, and textures. Interior decorators, designers, and builders were quick to install these tile products in other areas of the house: the living room, hallway, family room, dining room, and even the bedroom. Today, home owners realize that ceramic tiles offer a low-maintenance alternative to other traditional building materials and, with the vast assortment of tiles to choose from, they are limited only by their imagination when it comes to decorating their homes.

1–5 (opposite page). *A simple but effective pattern is used in this historic building. The floor serves as a unifying element that brings together the elaborate ceiling and grand architectural features: the arches, marble stairs, and wall pilasters. Admittedly most residential homes are not as grandiose as this structure. Still the problems of design and focal harmony, as well as function, are present in all homes, albeit on a smaller scale.*

2–1. *Tiles are manufactured with a wide variety of shapes, colors, and textures. They can be used to create dramatic or subtle decorative effects. Here, for example, the tiles are all the same color but have different shapes and profiles. They create a look that suggests traditional, old world charm.* **(Photo courtesy of M.E. Tile Company)**

All About Tiles

HOW TILES ARE MADE

Modern tiles are made by shaping clay. Nature produces the clay by decomposing rocks. In some instances, the clay may be used as it is dug from the ground, but it is seldom found free of other minerals. It usually contains amounts of silicates such as quartz or sand. When these are removed by washing, the clay appears in its purest form, called kaolin, which is an aluminum silicate.

The desirable property of kaolin is its plasticity. When mixed with water, it can be molded into various shapes, and it will retain that relative shape as it dries. As admirable as this plasticity is, it has some disadvantages. As the water evaporates from pure kaolin, the tiles will shrink somewhat, so extenders such as gypsum or talc are added. These clays are called "lean," and they need less water in the shaping process, so they shrink less as they dry. In contrast, "fat" clays—those that are more plastic—need more water to make them workable. They shrink more as they dry, and often break or crack if they dry too quickly.

In addition, kaolin may be mixed with other materials such as ground shale or feldspar to give it texture. Still other products, often metal compounds, are added to give the clay color that can range from an off-white to gray, beige, or earthen hues.

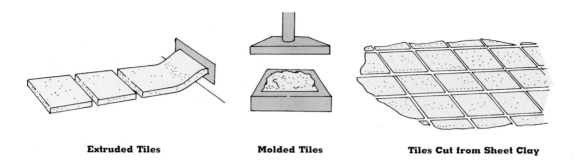

Extruded Tiles   **Molded Tiles**   **Tiles Cut from Sheet Clay**

2–2. *There are a number of ways tile makers can shape clay into a bisque. The clay can be extruded through a form into an extended ribbon and then sliced to length. The clay can be packed into a mold in a process called "dust-pressing." The clay can also be rolled into a sheet and then cut into individual pieces.*

After the clay is processed, it is mixed with water, shaped into a biscuit, commonly called a "green" bisque (the term "green" refers to an unfired tile), and then fired. There are a number of ways tile makers can shape clay into a bisque **(2–2)**. The clay can be extruded through a form into an extended ribbon, and then sliced to thickness. This method is often used for unglazed tiles.

Clay can also be packed into a mold to form bisques. This process is often called "dust-pressing" and is used by manufacturers who mass-produce tile. They use this method because there is little waste and less water is needed to form the clay. Another way to form tiles is by rolling the clay into a sheet and then cutting it, cookie-cutter style, into individual shapes.

Small shops that produce short runs of tiles with unusual colors, designs, or shapes do not have the heavy hydraulic presses or other machinery needed to force the clay into shape. Instead, they may cut the bisques or form them in a mold by hand. These handmade tiles are often more irregular in size, color, and thickness than the mass-produced tiles. However, these idiosyncrasies give the hand-

made tile a charm and rustic appeal that many people find appealing. As quaint and desirable as these "charming" tiles may be, they are also more costly and can be difficult to match should one become broken or damaged.

After the tiles are shaped, they are left to dry. When most of the water has evaporated, they are fired. Some tiles receive multiple firings, but most are fired only once. However, the time for this single firing may vary, depending upon the type of tile being made. Some tiles may receive a quick firing lasting only a few minutes, while others may remain in the kiln for a week.

Kiln temperatures can vary between 900° F and 2,500° F. In most cases, however, tiles will be fired at temperatures between 1,900° F and 2,200° F. Hotter temperatures and longer firing times produce tiles that are hard, strong, and almost impervious to water absorption. Conversely, tiles with limited firing time at low temperatures tend to be porous and water absorbent.

In major industrial areas, the kilns are fired with natural gas. Smaller kilns may use propane, wood, or electricity as fuel. A few Spanish and Italian kilns actually use olive pits as fuel! In some remote regions of Mexico, the kilns are made from the bodies of old automobiles and fueled with burning tires. Even though different fuels can affect appearance and sometimes the properties of the tile, most tile installers are not concerned with either the firing times or the kiln fuels. They are only interested in the final product, for example, the individual tiles.

Tiles are often glazed to enhance their appearance and give them greater durability. The glaze consists of silicates (the main ingredient of glass) and metal oxides. The oxides are essentially pigments that not only color the glaze but may also make it translucent or opaque. Most glazes are smooth, but sometimes ingredients may be added to give them texture. For example, when sawdust is added to the glaze, it burns away during the firing, leaving behind an irregular surface with tiny pockmarks. Other materials such as carbide particles can be added to give the tiles a rough, nonslip surface.

Even though a tile may seem hard and solid, it can have a number of air pockets throughout its cross section. These air pockets can affect how dense or permeable that tile will be. Tiles with a high percentage of air pockets are more porous and readily absorb water than those with fewer pockets. In an effort to establish some standards for tiles, the American National Standards Institute (ANSI) has devised a rating system for tile permeability and density.

TILE CATEGORIES

Tiles are measured by comparing a sample of the dry tile to one that has been boiled in water for five hours. As a result of these tests,

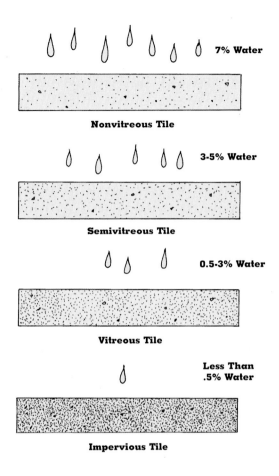

2–3. *The density of a tile will determine how much water it will absorb. Nonvitreous tiles are the least dense and will absorb as much as 7 percent water. Semivitreous tiles, being more dense than vitreous tiles, will absorb less water, about 3 to 5 percent. Vitreous tiles are relatively dense and will only absorb between 0.5 to 3 percent water. Impervious tiles have a water-absorption rate of less than 0.5 percent.*

the ANSI has set up four categories of tile: nonvitreous, semivitreous, vitreous, and impervious **(2–3)**. These categories are important to the tile setter because they give an indication as to how well the tile will perform in wet installations. A nonvitreous tile, for example, is porous and soaks up water and, therefore, would not be a good choice for a wet area like a shower. Each is described below.

Nonvitreous tiles receive short firings at low temperatures, so they are also cheaper than the tiles in other categories, but they are less dense and will absorb as much as 7 percent water. This makes nonvitreous tiles undesirable in wet installations and in outdoor locations where freezing temperatures can cause the internal moisture to expand and crack the tile.

In addition, nonvitreous tiles should be sprayed with a fine mist before grouting. This will prevent the tiles from drawing excess water from the grout before it has time to cure properly.

Semivitreous tiles are fired at a low temperature, but for longer durations than nonvitreous tiles. They are denser than nonvitreous tiles and will not absorb as much water (about 3 to 5 percent). They are not a good choice for outdoor locations, but can be used in wet locations if a waterproof sealer is applied. Like nonvitreous tiles, they should also be misted before applying grout.

Vitreous tiles are fired at temperatures of 2,200° F for as long as 30 hours. This extended firing makes the tiles relatively dense, so they have a water-absorption rate between 0.5 and 3 percent. This absorption capacity makes vitreous tiles a good choice for wet installations or in areas subject to freezing. In addition, their density gives them a greater compression strength so they can be used in floor installations.

Impervious tiles have a water-absorption rate of less than 0.5 percent. This low absorption rate makes them almost waterproof, so they can be used in all wet installations. Since they can withstand repeated cleaning and sterilization treatments, they are frequently used in hospitals and pharmaceutical rooms.

While impervious tiles may seem like an ideal product, they have a downside. Due to their extreme density, more effort is required to cut and trim them.

GLAZE HARDNESS

Glazes also have a hardness rating scale, but few installers concern themselves with it, because not all manufacturers include it in their specifications. The ratings are based on the Mohs' scale. It measures the hardness of the glaze and is determined by the type of material needed to scratch the glaze. The Mohs' ratings range from 1, the softest surface that can be scratched by talc, to 10, the hardest, which can only be scratched by a diamond.

The hardness scale can be a good indication of a tile's suitability for an installation (provided, of course, that it is included in the specifications). For example, a tile glaze with a hardness rating of 3 or 4 is relatively soft and will not withstand much wear. It is suitable for wall installations. A rating of 5 or 6 can be used for floors that receive normal traffic, while a glaze with a 7 or 8 can be used on floors that see heavy traffic.

TILE TYPES

Most tile manufacturers use a common terminology to identify their products. Unfortunately, the terms are not exact and are often used loosely to describe products that can be similar or even widely different. In addition, it is sometimes difficult to apply the terms accurately to newer products that use the latest materials or ingredients. Still, anyone interested in purchasing and/or installing tiles should be acquainted with the tile terminology because it will help in communicating with the tile dealer.

The categories of tile include: pavers, quarry tiles, mosaics, glazed wall tiles, and cement-bodied tiles. *Pavers* are usually made by the dust-pressed method **(2–4)**. They range in size from 6 to 12 inches square, may be glazed or unglazed, and can be up to $^3/_4$ inch thick. They are produced mainly for floors, but for decorative purposes they can also be installed on walls. Machine-made pavers are fired at high temperatures, making them vitreous or semivitreous.

Some handmade pavers, often made in Mexico, are fired at low temperatures, producing a nonvitreous product. They are used mainly for floors, but because they vary in thickness, extra care must be taken in installation to ensure a relatively even surface. Before installation, the backs of these pavers should be brushed clean, and then rinsed with clear water. Allow the tiles to dry before installing them.

Manufactured pavers are usually sealed. The sealer makes grouting easier and protects the tiles from excessive wear and from staining. Handmade pavers may not be sealed, so it is important to apply a sealer made especially for tiles.

Quarry tiles were originally cut from quarried stone, and then surfaced and polished. The final product had a uniform dimension. The term has been expanded to include semivitreous or vitreous clay tiles made by extrusion. These tiles are usually fired unglazed (some, however, may receive a glaze) so they resemble the original stone quarry tiles. Their compression strength makes them suitable for floor

2–4. *This floor installation uses large pavers with smaller pieces at corner points. The design is simple but effective. Still it requires careful planning to make the two different-sized pieces fit perfectly together. An additional visual accent is provided by the patterned border tiles. The pattern is echoed in some of the smaller corner tiles.* **(Photo courtesy of Dal-Tile Company)**

installations, and because they are vitreous, they can be used in wet locations.

Quarry tiles range in size from 4 to 12 inches square and in thickness from $^1/_2$ to $^3/_4$ inch. They are also available in a variety of shapes: square, rectangular, and hexagonal.

They are not always sealed, but because of their density, sealing is not usually necessary.

Mosaic tiles are pieces less than 2 inches square (a few manufacturers label their product "mosaic" if the tiles are less than 6 inches square). They are usually made by the dust-pressed method with clay or porcelain, although traditionally a mosaic could also be composed of pieces of glass, stone, pebbles, or even shells.

Generally, mosaic tile is available in 1- or 2-inch squares, 1 X 2-inch rectangles, or in hexagons. A few tile dealers stock loose tiles, but in most cases the tiles are sold as units mounted on a backing sheet. These sheets are approximately 12 inches square or larger. The sheet is a plastic or paper mesh that is left in place when the tile is set.

Mosaic tiles are very dense; hence, they are vitreous and are suitable for wet and freeze/thaw installations. They can be used for floors, countertops, and walls.

Glazed wall tiles are made by the dust-press method. They are generally about $1/4$ inch thick and range in size from 4 X 4 to 6 X 6 inches. The tiles are made with soft clay and glaze, so they are not as durable as pavers, quarry, or mosaic tiles, and are unsuitable for floor use. They can be used for wet installations; they are manufactured for indoor use only because they are not stable in freeze/thaw conditions.

Cement-bodied tiles are made not of clay, but of extruded mortar. They are less expensive than regular tiles because the firing time is restricted to drying the tiles, not hardening them. Cement-bodied tiles are not glazed, but an earth-tone colorant is sometimes added after hardening. In addition, the manufacturer may apply a sealer to the tiles to improve durability. These tiles are often texturized by stamping a pattern into the face of the tile before it is fired.

This tile has good compression strength and wears well, so it is a good choice for floor installations. It is not recommended for either wet installations or outdoor locations.

During the manufacturing process, a selvage edge is created around the perimeter of the cement-bodied tile. Usually, but not always, this is removed by the manufacturer prior to packaging and shipping. In some cases, the selvage edge may still be present; then it should be trimmed or ground off prior to installation. While cement-bodied tiles can be cut with the snap cutter, the wet saw gives a better cut. *(Refer to Chapter 3 for information on tools.)*

TILE GRADES

In a effort to give the installer and consumer more guidelines for choosing tiles and at the same time create greater standards for quality control, the ANSI (American National Standards Institute) developed a grading system for tiles sold in the United States. According to the ANSI system, there are three tile grades: standard grade, second grade, and decorative thin wall tile.

Standard-grade tile meets all the minimum specifications set for tile by the ANSI. *Second-grade tile* has the structural integrity of the standard-grade product, but it has minor imperfections in the glaze and the actual dimensions may vary from the nominal size. Often second-grade tiles are part of the setup or "first-of-the-run" or they may be "last-of-the-run" pieces of a mass-produced lot. *Decorative tile* is more fragile and should be

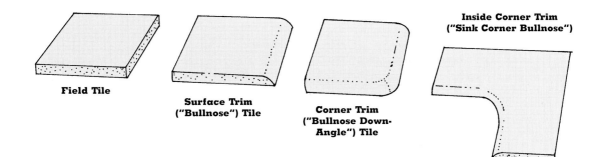

2–5. *Tiles for a flat surface come in various shapes. Field tiles are flat tiles used in the center of an installation. Surface trim tiles, also called "bullnose" tiles, have one edge rounded over. These are designed to be positioned along the edge of an installation. Trim tiles with two rounded edges are used on the corners of an installation. These are also called "surface trim down-angle tiles." Surface tiles are also made to finish an inside corner—these are common on sink countertops. They have two inside finished sides and are sometimes called "sink-corner surface trim tiles."*

used only for decorative, rather than functional, purposes.

Because this grading system is somewhat broad, the Porcelain Enamel Institute created a system that is more exacting. It gives the consumer a more precise guide for product application. Called the PEI Wear Rating System, it divides tile into five groups.

Group I tiles are suitable for use in home bathrooms exposed to medium traffic with soft footwear.

Group II tiles are suitable for use in home areas that receive a medium amount of traffic. Group II tiles should not be used in either kitchens or entrance foyers.

Group III tiles are suitable for all residential areas and light commercial applications.

Group IV tiles are made for use in medium commercial applications and light institutional (restaurants or hotel lobbies) installations.

Group V tiles are durable tiles that can be used for exterior applications, in wet areas, or in areas of heavy traffic.

FIELD AND TRIM TILES

Tiles that occupy the main area of a design are called *field tiles* **(2–5)**. Field tiles that are glazed have the glaze on the surface, not on the ends. Tiles that fit around the edges of the field as either end or border pieces are called *trim tiles* (refer to **2–5**). Because one or more edges of the individual trim tiles are exposed, the edges as well as the top surface may have a glaze. Trim tile configuration—that is, the shape and number of glaze edges—fits into two categories: surface trim and radius trim.

Surface trim tiles (refer to **2–5**) are designed to fit around the perimeter of the field tiles. The field tiles may be installed as a wainscoting[1] or a backsplash.[2] The trim tiles would then finish off the top or side edges. In many installations, two edges, a vertical and horizontal, will come together. Here, a special surface trim tile can be set to finish the corner. Called a *surface trim down tile* (refer to **2–5**), it

1. Wainscoting is the paneled lining along the lower part of an interior wall. **2.** A backsplash is a vertical surface that is designed to protect the wall behind a stove or countertop.

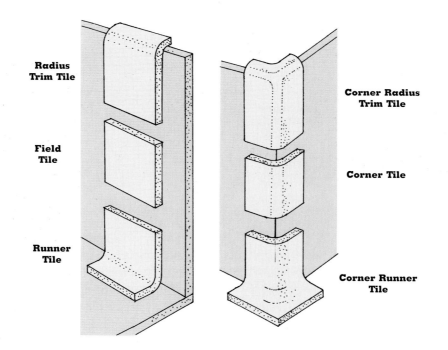

2–6. *Radius trim tiles are used when the wall or floor surface is on two levels. They have a finished, curved edge that will wrap around the raised surface. Radius trim tiles are available in a variety of shapes to fit around corners or for base trim (often called "runners").*

has two glazed edges and a rounded corner so it neatly completes an outside corner.

For inside corners, there are trim tiles called *sink-corner surface trim tiles.* These tiles are bent at a right angle with the finished edges on the inside corner. Of course, as an alternative to the sink-corner tiles, it is also possible to miter two straight pieces of surface trim so they fit together as an inside corner.

Radius trim tiles **(2–6)** are designed to extend below the tile surface and cover the edge of the surface bed. Not all tile installations will be flush with the surrounding surface; in some cases, the tiles will be raised around the setting bed. This often happens when backer board is mounted over an existing drywall surface. Another use for radius

trim tiles is around the perimeter of counters. In these applications, the radius trim tiles form a rounded corner that overlaps the edge and completes the effect of the field tiles.

Radius trim tiles have one or more edges that curve down to cover the projecting surface bed. Like surface trim tiles, they are available in different shapes to cover straight edges and inside and outside corners. In addition to the common radius trim tile, which is basically a field tile with a curved edge, there is the *quarter-round radius trim.* Quarter-round radius trim tiles are essentially the rounded edge of the common radius trim tile without the body of the field tile. Both common and quarter-round radius trim tiles are used for straight runs.

For outside corners, there are *radius down-angle tiles.* Inside corners can be finished with *up-angle tiles* or *quarter-round sink-corner tiles.* Again, another solution to finishing the inside corner is to miter two pieces of radius trim to form the corner.

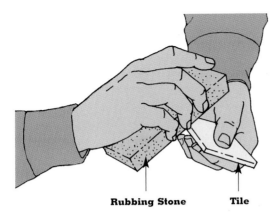

Rubbing Stone · **Tile**

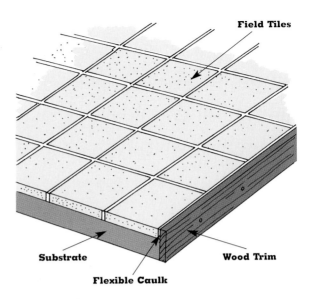

Field Tiles

Substrate · **Wood Trim** · **Flexible Caulk**

2–7. *Hand-cut tiles may have sharp or irregular, unsightly edges. These can be smoothed with a handheld rubbing stone. This task can also be done with carbide sandpaper.*

Unfortunately, not all manufacturers offer a full line of tiles for every need. If a brand of field tile does not offer the necessary trim tiles, there are a number of alternatives. Sometimes trim tiles can be found in similar or complementary colors that will work as well. Trim tiles can sometimes be hand-made by rounding the edges of field tiles with a handheld rubbing stone or carbide sandpaper **(2–7)**. This technique will work only with unglazed, soft-bodied field tiles.

2–8. *It is not always necessary to finish the edge of an installation with tiles. Edges can be finished with other materials like wood or metal. The joint between the tiles and the edging material should be filled with flexible caulk, not grout.*

Finally, the edges of the tile can be finished with another material such as wood or metal **(2–8)**. Using a dissimilar material with the tile can present a few problems, particularly in wet installations. Wood will expand if it gets wet; the tile will not. The joint between the two materials should be filled with flexible caulk, not grout, because the grout would only crack and disintegrate as the wood expands.

2-9. *Generally, people think of tiles for wall, floor, and kitchen countertop installations, but they can also be used to give a decorative accent to a common piece of furniture. Here green ceramic tiles are used to decorate a traditional cupboard. In addition to aesthetics, the tiles create a durable work surface within the soft pine cabinet top.* **(Photo courtesy of Lis King Tile Company)**

3–1. *Tile installation is not particularly difficult; nor does it require a lot of sophisticated tools. The few specialized tools that are required can usually be rented at a tool rental store or sometimes from a tile dealer. Measuring and marking tools are essential to ensure a quality installation. This floor using 12-inch, variegated green tiles looks good because the installation was carefully planned and laid out.*

Tile Tools and Materials

MEASURING AND MARKING TOOLS

A good set of tools is essential if you want to do a first-class job. Start by acquiring a complement of measuring and marking tools (**3–2** and **3–3**). There may be the temptation to get by with makeshift tools found around the home, like a yardstick and a tape measure, but these tools are not very accurate and accuracy is imperative when laying out the job.

A good *steel tape measure with a hooked end* is necessary. If you plan to use an old tape that has been around for a number of years, check it for accuracy by holding it against a flat steel scale.

Next, add a pair of *straightedges*, 36 and 48 inches long, to the tool kit. These can be made by cutting a true edge out of a strip of plywood, but aluminum edges from channel or angle stock will be more durable and easier to handle. At the risk of stressing the obvious, the straightedges must be absolutely straight. Periodically check their quality by laying them on a flat surface or by sighting along the edge.

A good layout depends on making lines that are not only straight but also plumb. For this a *spirit level* and a *plumb bob* are needed. The most practical spirit level for tile work should be 18 inches long and made of aluminum—it's lightweight and easy to clean. If

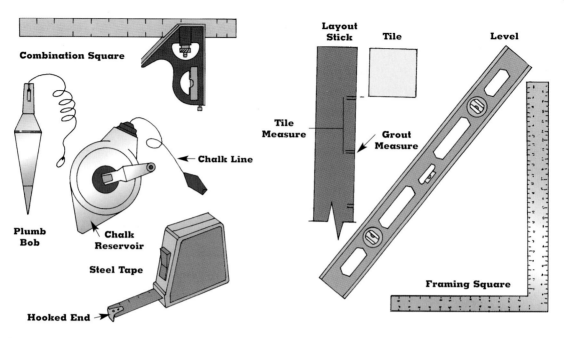

3–2. *For measuring and layout work, a quality steel tape measure with a hooked end is needed. A plumb bob is used for checking the accuracy of vertical surfaces. The chalk line is useful for putting straight lines along a surface. In addition to the cord, a professional chalk line has a reservoir to hold chalk dust. When the line is pulled from the reservoir, it is already chalked and ready to use. A combination square is useful for marking right angles and miter angles.*

3–3. *A large carpenter's framing square is best for making and checking right angles on a layout. A spirit level is essential to check that all surfaces are true and level. For tile installations, the level should be at least 18 inches long. An aluminum level can also be used as a straightedge. Another useful marking tool is a layout stick. It is possible to make one by marking a flat board with the widths of the tiles plus the widths of the grout joints.*

a longer level is needed, you can improvise by taping this one to a straightedge.

The plumb bob is simply a weight attached to a long cord. While almost any weight can be used, the commercially made bob weights taper to a point for greater accuracy. The plumb bob is only needed for checking the accuracy of vertical surfaces. It is not needed for floor work.

For setting right angles, at least one square is needed. Buy a large *carpenter's framing square*, and, if possible, add a *combination square*.

While working on the job, be sure to keep all measuring tools clean and free of mastic or mortar. Deposits of these substances can affect the accuracy of the tools. Also

make an effort not to drop these tools; this could also throw off their accuracy.

For marking on light surfaces, use an ordinary *soft lead pencil* or a *fine-line black marker*. On dark surfaces, use a *white* or *yellow pencil*. Another tool that is useful for layout work is a *chalk line*. A chalk line can be made by running chalk over a cord, but a professional model has a case that houses the line and a reservoir of chalk dust. A felt gasket in the case distributes chalk evenly over the line, so it is always ready to use. This can be a real time-saver on the job.

Another tool that can be very useful is a *layout stick*. Also called a *story* or *jury* pole, it is a relatively inexpensive tool because it is homemade. It is simply a flat piece of wood about $\frac{1}{4}$ inch thick and two to three inches wide. The length will vary depending on the field of tiles that will be installed; in general layout, sticks are about four to six feet long. Basically the stick will be divided up into a series of tile units. *A tile unit* is the width of one full tile plus a grout joint. The layout stick may be 5, 6, or even 10 tile units long.

If, for example, you were installing 6-inch tiles with a $\frac{1}{4}$-inch joint between them, the tile unit would be $6\frac{1}{4}$ inches. For a row of 10 tiles, the layout stick would be $62\frac{1}{4}$ inches long: ten tiles would be 60 inches, plus $2\frac{1}{4}$ inches for the nine $\frac{1}{4}$-inch joints between each tile. The layout stick can, of course, be longer if a larger field of tiles will be set, but it should never be so long as to be unwieldy.

The layout stick described above would work well for square tiles, but suppose the tiles are rectangular with a length longer than the width. Which measurement would make up the tile unit? In this case, it would be useful to make up two layout sticks, one with the tile width as the unit, and one with the length as the unit.

The layout stick can be helpful in determining how many tiles will be needed to fit into a given area, and for positioning the center of the tile field in a room.

SETTING TOOLS

It may seem that spreading the adhesive on the "setting bed" is a relatively straightforward task, and it is, provided the adhesive is spread in a uniform layer over the entire substrate. The *spreading trowel* is able to do this because of its unique design **(3–4)**. Spreading trowels have V- or crenellated-shaped notches on at least two sides. These notches spread the adhesives in a series of rows at a uniform depth and width. Ideally, the adhesive depth should be about two-thirds the thickness of the tile.

To change the thickness of the adhesive, it is only a matter of switching to a trowel with a larger or smaller notch configuration. To test if the adhesive depth is correct, spread a small quantity onto a flat surface and then press a tile into it. Remove the tile and examine the back. If the entire back is not completely covered with adhesive, then the depth needs to be increased. If, however, the adhesive covers the tile back and also exudes up around the sides, the adhesive layer is too thick.

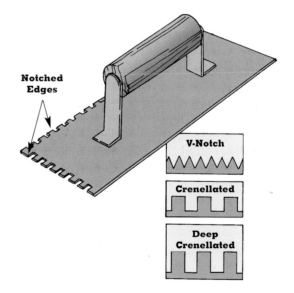

3–4. *A spreading trowel is essential for putting down an even coat of adhesive on the substrate. Spreading trowels have notched edges for spreading the adhesive in a series of rows at an even depth and width. The notched pattern may vary according to the needs of the installation. A V-notched trowel is recommended for installing mosaic tiles. A trowel with crenellated $\frac{1}{4}$ x $\frac{1}{4}$ x $\frac{1}{4}$-inch notches is best for installation of standard wall or quarry tiles. Trowels with deeper crenellated $\frac{3}{8}$-inch notches are good for laying down vitreous and natural stone tiles.*

Manufacturers sometimes specify the preferred tooth configuration for spreading their product, because adhesive coverage will vary with the size and shape of the trowel teeth. For example, when installing ceramic mosaic tiles, a $^5/_{32}$-inch V-notch trowel is recommended; for standard wall or quarry tile up to 6 inches, a $^1/_4$ X $^1/_4$ X $^1/_4$-inch-square-notch trowel; and for ceramic, vitreous, and natural stone tiles, use a $^1/_4$ X $^3/_8$ X $^1/_4$-inch square-notch trowel.

There are, of course, top-of-the-line notched trowels for professional use, but the one-time tile setter can often get by with inexpensive plastic models available at most home centers.

Another important, though unsophisticated, tool for setting tiles is called a *beating block*. Essentially it is a block of wood about 6 X 10 inches. Commercial beating blocks have rubber faces so the block will not scratch the tile face when positioned. The block is used to set the tiles and align them to the surrounding tiles. Simply place the block on the tile face and gently tap it with a rubber mallet.

The beating block should never be used on tiles with uneven faces (with one edge higher than the others), as this might cause an edge to pop up. Also, the beating block should never be used to set tiles in a shallow layer of adhesive.

Not all tile setters use the beating block; some prefer to push with their fingers or even pound with their hands on the tiles. This may be a little tough on the hands, but it will ensure that the tiles will not be damaged while simultaneously offering greater control because the setter can actually feel how much force is being applied to the tiles.

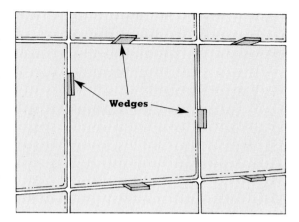

3–5. *Wedges are small pieces of plastic that are positioned between the tiles to ensure a consistent gap for the grout. Generally they are left in place at least until the adhesive sets enough to hold the tiles without slipping—usually about 24 hours.*

Wedges and *spacers* are small pieces of extruded plastic that are positioned to ensure a consistent gap between the tiles **(3–5)**. The wedges are used to gap vertical tiles; the spacers can be fit between horizontal or vertical tiles. Generally they are left in place at least until the adhesive sets enough to hold the tiles without slipping—ideally about 24 hours.

Some installers leave the spacers in permanently and grout over them. This, however, has its drawbacks: the grout layer over the spacers will be thinner than that in the surrounding areas and noticeably lighter in color (this effect is called "ghosting").

Not all tile jobs require the use of spacers. Many tiles have *spacer tabs* built onto their edges. Here the tiles can be butted up against each other, and the spacer pieces will maintain a gap between them. While this sounds ideal, it still requires judgment and attention to detail on the part of the installer. Not all the spacer tabs are the same size. This happens because some tiles shrink a little more than others as they are being fired. The tile setter must inspect each tile carefully as it is put into position.

Tiles that are too close can be nudged apart to compensate for the uneven spacer tabs. In this instance, wedges are very useful. They can be inserted between the tiles to open up the gap, and they are ideal for this task because their tapered shape allows the setter to space the gap in minute increments to ensure perfect alignment with the neighboring tiles. Like the spacers, they are left in place until the adhesive cures and then removed (unlike the spacers, they cannot be left in place because they protrude beyond the face of the tile). In this way, the gap will be maintained.

TILE-CUTTING TOOLS

Not all tiles can be put down intact. Sometimes it will be necessary to place tiles around plumbing or in narrow spaces. Obviously the tiles will have to be cut or shaped to fit into these areas.

Tile nippers, also called *biters,* are used to nibble away bits of tile and shape the piece so it can fit around plumbing valves, door casings, or flanges **(3–6)**. Nippers are plier-like tools that come in various sizes with different jaw configurations. The tile is gripped in the carbide-tipped jaws; downward pressure exerted on the handles causes bits of tile to snap off.

Nippers are useful for cutting irregular shapes from a tile, but they leave a jagged edge so they are not used for making straight cuts. For these cuts, the tool of choice is the *snap cutter.* Strictly speaking, the term "cutter" is a misnomer, because the tool does not actually cut the tile. Instead it breaks it along a scored line.

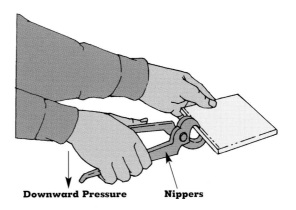

Downward Pressure   **Nippers**

3–6. *Tile nippers are plier-like tools that can be useful for cutting irregular shapes, like a notch in a tile to accommodate a protruding pipe, or for trimming the edges of a tile. The tile is gripped in the carbide-tipped jaws. Exerting downward pressure causes bits of the tile to snap off.*

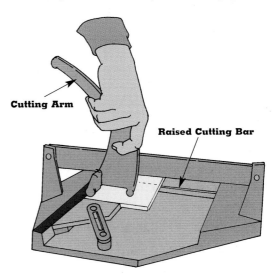

Cutting Arm

Raised Cutting Bar

3–7. *Snap cutters are available in various configurations, but they utilize the same cutting principle. The tile is placed on the cutting bed and held in place. In the center of the bed is a raised bar. The tile is placed on the bar. Pressing down on the cutting arm puts pressure on the edges of the tile and breaks it in two.*

Snap cutters are available in various configurations, but they utilize the same cutting principle **(3–7)**. The tile is placed on the cutting bed and held in place. In the center of the bed is a raised bar, the cutting bar. The tile

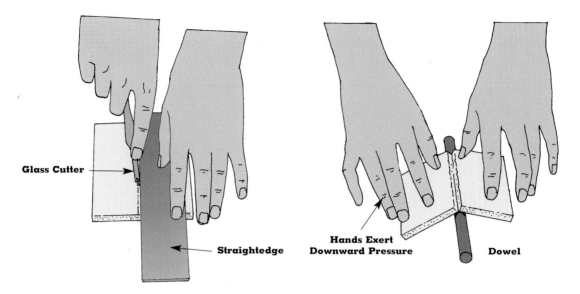

3–8 and **3–9.** *Tiles can also be snapped by hand. First make a score line across the face of the tile with a glass cutter and straightedge. Then position the tile over a large nail or dowel, score side up. Align the tile so the line is directly over the dowel, and then press down the edges of the tile with both hands. The tile should break clean at the score line.*

is positioned on the *cutting bar*. A sharp cutting wheel is drawn across the tile face. The wheel does not cut the tile, but only scores the surface. Pressing down on the cutting arm puts pressure on the edges of the tile. On either side of this bar are soft rubber pads that "give" when pressure is applied. The pressure on the tile ends makes it snap at the breaking bar.

It is also possible to snap tiles with less sophisticated tools. The tile can be scored with a *glass cutter,* and then broken by positioning it over a large nail or dowel, scored side up **(3–8 and 3–9).** Align the tile so the scored line is directly over the nail, and then press down on the edges of the tile with both hands. The tile will break clean at the scored line. While this technique is effective for cutting small tiles, it can be difficult with thick tiles and it can be tedious and time-consuming if there are a large number of tiles to snap.

Another device for cutting tiles is a *cutting*

saw (also called a *wet saw*). This is the tool of choice for most professional tile setters because it cuts through the tiles like a table saw cuts through a wooden board. The tool actually cuts the tiles with a circular diamond blade **(3–10).** A water jet directed at the rotating blade cools it and washes away tile debris.

This tool is particularly effective for cutting thin pieces of tile ($1/2$ inch wide) or for cutting smooth edges that may be left exposed. The wet saw is essential for cutting tiles made of marble and stone. Both the cutting saw and tile snapper are expensive, but they can usually be rented at home centers or tile suppliers.

The cutting saw is a stationary, tabletop tool, but it is also possible to cut tile, or backer board, with a *hand grinder* that has been fitted with a diamond-blade saw **(3–11).** The cuts made with this tool are not as straight as those with the wet saw; still, it is useful to have it on hand for quick trimming and for touching up large pieces (particularly backer board) that would be unwieldy on the wet saw.

In addition to making straight or curved cuts, it is sometimes necessary to bore holes in the tiles or backer board so fixtures or plumbing can project through. The tool of choice for this task is the *carbide-tipped hole saw* (3–12). It chucks into an ordinary electric drill, and can cut holes in backer board and soft- and hard-bodied tiles.

Cutting holes in hard-bodied tiles with the hole saw can be slow and tedious work. As the saw bites deeper into the tile body, a considerable amount of heat will be generated. The excessive heat often causes the tile to crack or break. An easy way to prevent this and dissipate the heat is by submerging the tile under water during the cutting operation.

There is, however, a danger to this method. Obviously working around water with any electrical power tool poses a danger of electrocution to the operator. It is essential to keep the drill body and cord out of water, and to make sure that the tool is plugged into a ground fault circuit interrupter outlet. Also, make sure that you wear the proper attire, as discussed in Safety Considerations on pages 36 to 38.

Some professional tile installers use the wet saw to cut holes—more specifically, openings—in the center of tiles. They turn the tile face side down and make four cuts on the back of it. These cuts overlap to form a rectangle, similar to a tic-tac-toe grid. The trick is to make the cuts deep enough to come within $1/16$ inch or less of the face of the tile without breaking through. The tile is then flipped over and tapped on the face with a small hammer. These light blows must be delivered to the opposite side of the rectangle. When properly hit, the rectangle will pop out, leaving a square hole in the center of the tile.

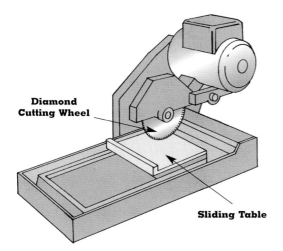

Diamond Cutting Wheel

Sliding Table

3–10. *The wet or cutting saw is the cutting tool of choice for most professional tile setters. It cuts through tiles like a table saw cuts through a wooden board. The saw is fitted with a diamond-cutting blade and a water jet directed at the blade keeps it cool during the cutting operation.*

3–11. *A hand grinder fitted with an abrasive cutting wheel can be used to cut tiles or cement backer board. When fitted with a grinding wheel, it can be used to dress or trim tile edges.* **(Photo courtesy of Sears, Roebuck and Company)**

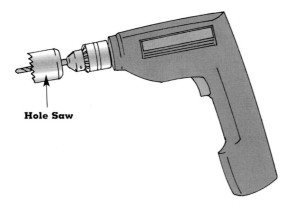

Hole Saw

3–12. *The best tool for making holes in tiles is an electric drill fitted with a carbide-tipped hole saw.*

This method takes a little practice, and the hole is not as neat as one cut with a hole saw, but it's a little faster. The opening is also rather crude in comparison to the hole-saw cut, so it must also be covered with an escutcheon or faceplate.

GROUT TOOLS

Grout trowels are stiff trowels with rubber faces **(3–13)**. They are used for pushing the grout into the gaps between the tiles and for removing excess grout. There are two types of grout trowel. One model has a hard rubber face. It is used for grouting floor tiles. The other type has a softer face, sometimes with a foam backing, and is designed for grouting tiles with glazed faces. In addition to packing the grout into the gaps, the trowel can be used on edge to scrape away excess grout.

The grout must be removed from the tile face before it has a chance to harden. The best tool for this is a *grout sponge*. It looks like a large kitchen sponge except it has rounded edges and corners. The rounded edges make it easy to smooth the gaps without gouging the grout out. Other grout-cleaning tools include a *plastic abrasive pad* (one brand is Scotch-Brite) and *cheesecloth*. Steel wool should never be used to clean grout from tiles, because the steel particles can easily break off and become lodged in the grout. Eventually they will rust and discolor the grout.

Another tool that is sometimes used to pack grout is a *grout bag* **(3–14)**. The bag looks like a chef's pastry bag, and is used in much the same way. Grout is loaded into the bag. The bag is then squeezed until grout is extruded from the tip, where it may be directed into the gaps.

MISCELLANEOUS TOOLS

The tools described above are the standard items for a straightforward tile installation. If you observe professional tile installers—or indeed, any professionals at work—you will probably notice that they frequently make or improvise their own tools. Since straight lines are an important, and indeed an essential, part of the final installation, many tile installers frequently make their own straightedges to various lengths by buying aluminum in angle stock (angle stock is less likely to bend and distort then bar stock) and then cutting it to a variety of lengths. In this way, they have a straightedge handy for almost any installation.

If you plan to rent any tools, like a wet saw, it is worth your time to look through the rental dealer's catalog to see if there are any other tools available that could possibly save time and labor. For example, a *power mixer* could be rented. This is simply a wand that is chucked into a heavy-duty drill (both are usually rented as one unit). This can be handy

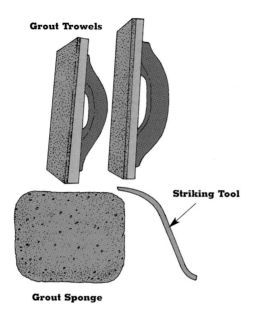

Grout Trowels

Striking Tool

Grout Sponge

3–13. *Grout trowels are stiff, usually made of wood, with rubber faces. They are used to push the grout into the gaps between the tiles and also to remove excess grout. One type of grout trowel has a hard rubber face. It is used for grouting floor tiles. Grout trowels with soft rubber faces are designed for grouting tiles with glazed faces. The grout sponge is used to remove grout from the tile face. It has rounded edges and corners for smoothing the grout without making gouges. Another tool that is useful for smoothing grout is the striking tool. It is simply a piece of round bar stock with curved ends. Dragging it along the gap will smooth the grout.*

if you plan to do a large installation and will have to mix a lot of adhesive. Do not attempt to mix adhesive with a small ¼-inch drill. The adhesive is so thick that the drill motor could be overworked and burned out.

While this may not be practical for a single installation, it is still a time saver to have at least a custom-made straightedge to fit the job at hand. Unfortunately, few jobs are completely straightforward, and often some improvisation is required when work is in progress. Consider, for example, an existing tile surface that must be removed to install

new tiles. This comes under the category of demolition.

There are no hard and fast rules for demolition work; most do-it-yourselfers, and a large number of professionals, grab whatever tool is handy to get the job done. A screwdriver becomes a pry bar or a chisel, and a claw hammer becomes a mallet. The guideline here is: "If it works, then it must be okay!"

There are two problems with this approach. First, inappropriate use can ruin a good tool; second, using a tool for a use that it was not designed for can be a serious safety hazard. *Claw hammers*, for example, are not properly hardened to resist impacts with other metal tools. The heads can easily chip or shatter and send metal particles flying. It is far better to use a *ball peen hammer* (also called

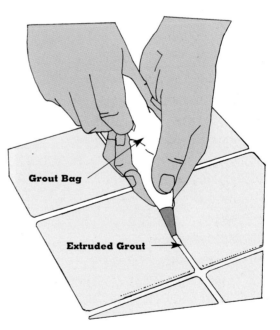

Grout Bag

Extruded Grout

3–14. *Another tool that is sometimes used to pack grout is a grout bag. The bag looks like a chef's pastry bag, and is used in much the same way. Grout is loaded into the bag and the bag is squeezed until grout extrudes from the tip where it may be directed into the gaps.*

a *machinist's hammer*) for this. And a *cold chisel* should be substituted for the screwdriver. This means that the do-it-yourselfer must acquire a number of new tools, but the end result will be a safer and better-looking job.

Installing tile may also involve tasks that have nothing to do with tile. It may be necessary, for example, to add supports to the wall framing or modify plumbing fixtures before the tiles can be set. These jobs fall under the category of carpentry and plumbing and will require special tools. It is not the scope of this book to cover either carpentry or plumbing techniques, so the reader will have to look elsewhere to find what tools are required for these jobs.

Finally, the most important tools are ones that cannot be bought. These are a pair of critical eyes and an organized mind. The best tile setters are the ones who take the time and effort to measure and work accurately, plan each installation carefully, and constantly check to be sure the tiles are properly aligned.

SAFETY CONSIDERATIONS

Modern technology and manufacturing has produced a number of fine products that make living more comfortable. Unfortunately, the tools and materials needed to install these products often create potential hazards. Tile installation is no exception. It might seem that because tiles are made from natural earth materials there would be little or no danger installing them. In theory this may be correct, but installation techniques often require the use of power tools. It is important to be thoroughly familiar with the operation and safety features of any power tool before attempting to use it. In addition, it is essential to wear proper safety equipment and gear when using any tool (**3–15 to 3–17**).

To prevent eye injuries, *safety goggles* are a must. Unfortunately most workers, professional and amateur alike, do not take the time to slip on a pair of goggles. Consequently, over half of the tool-related personal injuries reported in hospital emergency rooms are eye-related, and these are the most traumatic of all injuries. A few minutes devoted to donning safety gear can prevent a lifetime of anguish over a disfiguring accident.

A *dust mask* will protect the wearer from inhaling tile dust, but does not offer protection against toxic vapors. Here it is essential to have a good respirator; it should have a seal of approval from either the Occupational Safety and Health Association (OSHA) or the National Institute of Occupational Safety and Health (NIOSH).

Finally, the safety wardrobe should include work gloves. *Rubber gloves* can protect the hands and arms from the effects of chemicals; *heavy-duty work gloves* will shield the hands from abrasive masonry and tile substances.

Electrical safety is another consideration. Since many tile jobs require working around water, for cooling and cleanup, it is vital to keep all electrical connections away from the water and also to use *ground-fault circuit-interrupter (GFCI) outlets* whenever possible.

Solvent-based adhesives and mastics are flammable, so using them presents a potential fire hazard. The work area should be well ventilated to allow toxic fumes to escape before they collect, and all open flames—including pilot lights on the stove and water heater—should be extinguished when applying these adhesives.

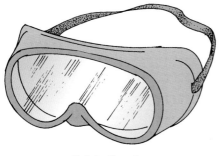

Safety Goggles

3–15. *To prevent eye injuries, safety goggles are a must. Unfortunately, most workers, professional as well as do-it-yourselfers, often neglect this item. As a result, almost half the tool-related personal injuries reported in hospital emergency rooms are eye-related, and these are the most traumatic of all injuries.*

While tiles may be relatively safe to handle, many of the adhesives used to mount them are not. Solvent-based mastics contain toluene; other adhesives contain xylene. These substances can produce harmful vapors and cause skin irritation. Even cutting into inert substances like cement and tile will release dust that can be harmful to inhale.

Unfortunately, not all manufacturers list the ingredients on their product labels. The safety-conscious worker would do well, then, to assume that all the products have some toxic ingredients and take adequate safety precautions by ensuring that the work area is adequately ventilated and all workers don protective gear.

Safety gear offers protection from toxins and flying particles; however, it is no substitute for working carefully and observing proper and safe working techniques. Do the following when working with power tools, glues, etc.:

1. Carefully read all container labels and follow manufacturer's recommendations and warnings for using the products and tools.

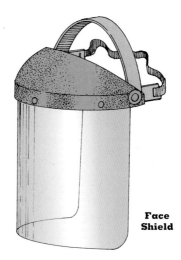

Face Shield

3–16. *Safety goggles are adequate for most work, but chiseling out broken tiles may call for greater protection. This task often sends sharp bits of tile flying up at the worker's face. A face shield offers more protection than safety goggles, since it protects the entire face as well as the eyes.*

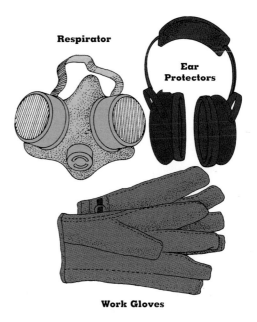

Respirator

Ear Protectors

Work Gloves

3–17. *Demolition work, cutting tiles, and mixing adhesives and grout can produce dust and flying particles. This type of work can also be hard on the hands. Working with power cutting tools can generate noise that can damage the ears. It is always a good practice to protect yourself by donning appropriate safety gear: goggles, ear protectors, a dust mask or respirator, and heavy-duty work gloves.*

2. Plug all electrical tools into grounded outlets.

3. Make sure all tools are sharp and in good working order.

4. Do not attempt to change a blade or drill bit unless the tool is unplugged.

5. Never overload a circuit, and never use an electric tool in or around wet locations.

6. Keep hands away from blades and other moving parts.

7. Wear snug-fitting clothing to avoid snags. Do not wear any jewelry or anything that can get caught by a moving blade.

8. Be alert when using any power tool and never operate it when tired or under the influence of medication.

9. Make sure that there is plenty of room to work and enough light to see what you are doing.

10. Clamp or secure small tiles and other workpieces when sawing or drilling them.

11. Check and observe all building codes and obtain all the necessary permits before starting any project.

12. In addition to personal safety, consider the environment. Be sure to dispose of all toxins and solvents in a safe and conscientious manner. This may require putting waste materials in suitable containers, affixing the proper labels to the containers, and taking them to disposal centers. (Check the Yellow Pages for the location of the nearest center.) Do not dump any toxins, solvents, or industrial-grade waste down the drain.

ADHESIVES
Thicksets
Traditionally, the method used to adhere tiles to a surface was to embed them in a prepared layer of mortar or portland cement. Mortar is a mixture of cement, lime, sand, and water. Portland cement (and indeed all cement) is a mixture of lime and clay mixed with water. The name "portland" probably comes from the way the cured cement resembles the hard stones of Portland, England.

The mortar or cement is prepared to a workable consistency and then troweled over a surface. Usually metal lath is secured to the surface first to ensure a firmer bond. The thickness of the mortar bed is approximately one inch; hence, it is referred to as a *thick bed* or *thickset*.

When the mortar bed is laid and is still pliable, a thin bond coat of portland cement is applied over the surface. The tiles are embedded in this and leveled with a beater block **(3–18)**.

Thickset provides an excellent base for heavy-duty surfaces, for example, those floors that will be subjected to heavy traffic and weight. It is also useful for leveling uneven surfaces. Unfortunately, it is difficult to apply properly and beyond the skills of novices and most do-it-yourselfers. Also, the thickset adhesive can be heavy and not all floors are sufficiently braced to hold the extra weight.

Thinsets
In an effort to make tile installation easier, manufacturers have developed another line of adhesives, called "thinsets" because they are spread in layers of about $1/8$ inch. Technically, any tile adhesive that is spread in a thin layer is a "thinset." Most tile setters, however, use the term "mastics" for the organic thinsets and reserve the term "thinset" for any other thin layer of adhesive.

The name "organic mastic" suggests an adhesive made of leaves and vegetable by-products, but these are actually compounds of hydrocarbon molecules. They have either a latex or petroleum base and consist of two elements: a bonding agent and a binder.

The bonding agent is the actual adhesive. The binder holds the bonding agent in suspension and determines the working properties (viscosity, drying time, etc.), and then evaporates, leaving the adhesive to cure. Petroleum-based mastics have a solvent binder; the binder in latex mastics is water. Since latex binders are nonflammable, they are a little safer to use, and are probably a better choice if you have allergies.

Organic mastics are the most popular adhesives, possibly because they are ready to use and are less expensive than thinset adhesives. They also begin to grip even before they are fully cured, so they work very well with vertical applications, such as tiling a wall.

Still, they have serious drawbacks and they are not a good choice for all jobs. The compressive strength is inferior to that of the thinsets. They are less flexible than the latex thinsets, so they require a completely flat and stable substrate. Since most of the organic mastics are not waterproof (be sure to read the specifications on the label to find out if the mastic is waterproof), they are not suitable for wet locations. Finally, most of the mastics are affected by heat and they should not be used in locations with heating appliances.

Thinset adhesives have much greater bonding and compression strength than organic mastics, but they must be mixed prior to use. They come in powdered form and must be mixed with water, liquid latex, or acrylic (called polymer modified thinsets), or epoxy resin. They set up more quickly than organic mastics and most are suitable in areas where heat or high temperatures may be a factor. They are also a good choice for wet applications.

The water-mix thinset adhesives are packaged in powder form and are available in 5-, 10-, 25-, and 50-pound bags. They can be mixed on site with pure water. Unfortunately,

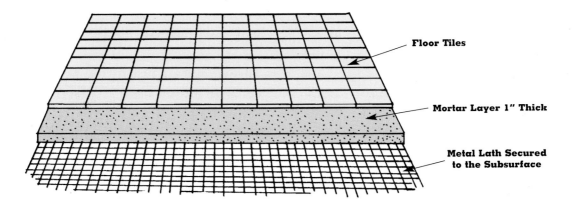

3–18. *Traditionally the method used to adhere tiles to a surface was to embed them in a prepared layer of mortar or portland cement. Metal lath is first secured to the substrate to ensure a good bond. The tiles are embedded in the wet cement with a beater block.*

not all water-based thinset can be applied on CBU (cementitious backer unit) or even plywood. It is important to carefully read the manufacturer's specifications before applying them.

Liquid latex and acrylic thinsets are less popular than the water-based thinsets because the powdered ingredients must be mixed with liquid polymer. This means carrying an extra container onto the job site. In an effort to overcome this difficulty, manufacturers developed a polymer powder that is added to the thinset powder. The tile installer only adds water to this mix, yet still gets the same quality polymer thinset.

Polymer thinsets have a greater compression strength and are more flexible than water-based thinsets. They are good adhesives to use in wet installations provided a proper waterproof underlayment has been installed.

Epoxy thinsets offer superior bonding strength and are a good choice when laying tiles on metal or plywood surfaces. Epoxy thinsets are composed of three parts: epoxy resin, hardener (both resin and hardener are the standard elements of all epoxy adhesives), and a filler powder.

Epoxy thinsets are of two types, and the difference lies in the composition of the filler powder. Regular epoxy adhesives have a filler powder of sand and portland cement and are used mainly for setting tiles. The other type of epoxy adhesive, commonly called 100 percent solids, has a filler base of silica sand and dyestuffs. In addition to being useful as a setting adhesive, it can also be used as a grout.

GROUT

After the adhesive has set and dried (drying time will vary with different brands of adhesive), the gaps between each tile are filled with grout. The grout keeps water, dirt, and moisture from penetrating under the tiles and destroying the adhesive bond beneath.

Grout is essentially a cement-based powder that is available in two different forms: sanded and nonsanded (also called plain grout). Sanded grout is formulated to expand and contract in gaps that are more than $1/16$ inch wide. The sand gives the grout added strength and flexibility. Nonsanded grout is formulated for the narrow $1/16$-inch gaps. Nonsanded grout is more rigid than sanded grout.

While most grouts are mixed with water, others use a latex additive. They are a little more expensive, but they are more flexible and are more resistant to water penetration.

Grout is also available with added colorants. Originally, colored grout was only available in tones of white, gray, or brown, but many manufacturers have a product line featuring a wide variety of color choices. There are no hard and fast rules for choosing a colored grout; in the end, color choice is a matter of taste. However, dark tiles generally look better with light-colored grout and vice versa. This dark-with-light combination effectively highlights the geometric design of the tile pattern.

CAULKS

Caulks are flexible joint compounds that are used to fill gaps between the tiled surface and another material, for example, around the edge of a bathtub. Caulks may be latex-, acrylic-, rubber-, or silicone-based. They are water-resistant, but will dry out over time;

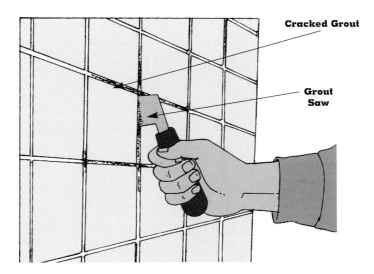

3–19. *If the grout between the tiles is beginning to crumble or crack, it should be replaced. Use a grout saw to rake out all of the old grout. Be careful not to damage the surrounding tiles. When the old grout is removed, new material can be installed.*

then they must be replaced. Caulks are stickier than grout compounds and are generally more difficult to apply and clean up, although some manufacturers offer a line of sanded caulk that is easier to use.

GROUT SEALERS

The primary purpose of a grout sealer is to make the grout less susceptible to staining, although a good sealer will also reduce mildew by preventing moisture from collecting. Applying a fresh coat of penetrating sealer annually can significantly extend the life of the grout.

REPAIRING TILE SURFACES

Even the best tile surfaces can develop problems. After a time, the grout may discolor or it may crack and fall out. If the grout is dirty or stained, but otherwise intact, it can usually be cleaned with a solution of phosphoric acid and water. Mix the solution according to the directions on the package (remember to add

the acid to the water, not water to the acid), apply it to the stained grout with a sponge, and then scrub with a nylon-bristle grout brush. For stubborn stains, the phosphoric acid may have to be applied full strength.

Phosphoric acid is not an especially harsh chemical, but it can irritate sensitive skin, so wear rubber gloves and eye protection. It can also etch glass; don't splash the solution on the glass shower doors.

If the grout is starting to crack or crumble, it should be replaced, but first the old grout will have to be removed **(3–19)**. This can be a tedious job, but using the proper tool, a grout saw, can make it easier. A grout saw has a short carbide-tipped blade that can rake out the old grout between the tiles. Move the saw back and forth to loosen and remove the grout, but be careful not to chip or damage the surrounding tiles.

Allow the tiles time to dry, and then mix a new batch of grout according to the package directions. For small areas, the grout can be forced into the gaps with a finger or a disposable plastic spatula. For larger areas, it's best to use a rubber grout float. Hold the float at a shallow angle and drag it across the tiles. Apply pressure to force the grout into the gaps.

Wait about 30 minutes for the grout to set, and then wipe the entire area with a round-cornered sponge. Work diagonally across the surface and then smooth the gaps with the sponge corner. Wait another hour, and then use a soft clean cloth to remove any remaining residue. After the grout has thoroughly dried (check the package specifications for recommended drying time), apply a coat of penetrating sealer.

Phosphoric acid, grout, grout saws, and other tiling supplies can be purchased at tile stores (look in the Yellow Pages under "Tile, Ceramic") or at home centers.

SUBSTRATE MATERIALS

The surface on which tiles are installed is often called the substrate. Theoretically, tiles can be mounted on almost any surface that is flat and rigid. These may sound like simple requirements, but they require some consideration. Being "perfectly flat" means that there cannot be any bumps or depressions, because rigid tiles cannot effectively bridge these defects and will break if pressure or weight is applied. The surface must also be level or, in the case of a vertical surface, plumb.

Rigidity is essential because tiles are inflexible. An insecure surface will bend when weight is applied, but the tiles will not. They will either break or pop off the underlying substrate.

Traditionally, tile setters bonded the tile to a sturdy mortar bed (called a "mud bed" by tile installers) that consisted of a $1\frac{1}{4}$-inch-thick layer of cement troweled over wire lath that was nailed to the boards above the framing. Today, builders use gypsum drywall or plywood as a backing in areas where moisture is not a problem. In bathrooms, showers, and other wet areas they install cement backer board.

Cementitious Backer Units

Cement backer board, also called CBU (cementitious backer unit), is a ready-made

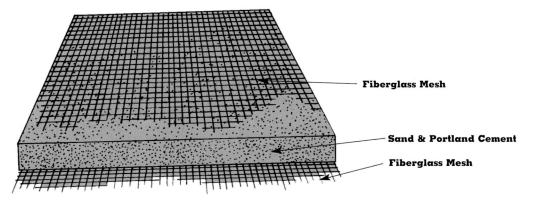

3–20. *Cement backer board, also called cementitous backer unit (abbreviated CBU), is a ready-made substrate that makes an ideal surface for tiling. It consists of a thin layer of sand and portland cement sandwiched between two layers of fiberglass mesh.*

substrate that makes an ideal surface for tiling **(3–20)**. The most common type of CBU consists of a thin layer of sand and portland cement sandwiched between two layers of fiberglass mesh. These boards are available in five thicknesses: $1/4$, $5/16$, $7/16$, $1/2$, and $5/8$ inch. Whenever possible, use the thickest board. The boards are available in sheets 32 and 48 inches wide and lengths up to 10 feet. They are more expensive than plywood, but unlike plywood they are relatively unaffected by moisture and are therefore ideal for wet areas.

Another type of CBU has a core of sand and portland cement, but the core also contains mineral fibers throughout. Because of the internal fibers, there is no need for a mesh layer (fiberglass webbing).

Even though CBUs are waterproof, they should be installed over a waterproof membrane when they will be used in wet areas. The membrane will protect the framing members beneath in the event of water seepage. *(See Chapter 5 for a discussion of waterproof membranes.)*

CBUs are dense, but they can be secured with a variety of common fasteners. They can be cut with special scribers or with a power saw fitted with a masonry blade.

While all CBUs look similar, they have different performance characteristics. Some, for example, are designed for interior use only. Not all CBUs carry a warranty. It is important to read the manufacturer's specifications to be sure that the product will perform adequately for your project.

It is usually a good idea to tape over all joints in CBU with fiberglass tape. The tape does more that simply conceal the joints (the tiles will obviously do this anyway). It

will also prevent any expansion in the joints from telegraphing into the tile surface above.

Gypsum Drywall

Gypsum drywall can be divided into two categories: regular drywall and moisture-resistant drywall (also called greenboard).

Regular drywall is the surfacing material commonly used for walls and ceilings in modern houses. While it can be used as a substrate for tile, it has two drawbacks. First, it is not waterproof and will soon deteriorate when used in wet areas, unless it is fitted with a waterproof membrane.

Second, unless it has firm support behind it, it is usually too flexible to support the rigid tiles properly. This, however, can be corrected by nailing a second layer of gypsum board directly over the first.

Even though moisture-resistant drywall is able to withstand humidity and moisture better than regular drywall, it is still not waterproof. It, too, will deteriorate after it has been exposed to repeated wetting. It should not be used in wet installations unless CBU is not available; even then it is necessary to install a waterproof membrane to protect it.

Plywood

Before the introduction of CBUs, plywood was a common substrate for many tile setters. While a number of tile floors with plywood underlayment have stood the test of time, almost an equal number have not. Problems occur because plywood is not always rigid or flat.

Setting floor tiles on a wood substrate presents special problems because the floor can bend and flex under weight. When tiles

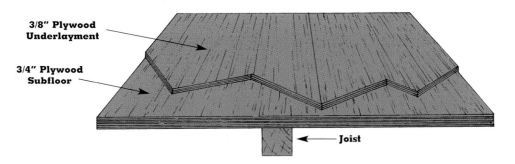

3–21. *Today most subfloors are of ³/₄-inch plywood. This may not be thick enough to support a tile floor. One way to add additional thickness and support is by nailing a layer of ³/₈-inch plywood to the subfloor.*

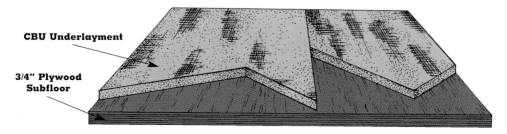

3–22. *A more rigid and substantial subfloor can be made by nailing CBU panels to the subfloor.*

are bonded to the substrate, the grout will crack and the tiles will pop loose unless the wood is thick enough to resist bending. Most subfloors are ³/₄-inch plywood (older floors may have 1 × 6-inch boards). This is not thick enough to support a tile floor. One way to add thickness is by nailing a layer of ³/₈-inch plywood (called the underlayment) to the subfloor **(3–21)**.

Even with the addition of a ³/₈-inch plywood underlayment, the floor may flex if it absorbs too much moisture. This is not a problem in areas where the humidity remains at comfortable levels, but in locations with high humidity levels the plywood can absorb too much moisture. When this happens, it will expand and warp. Obviously, an easy solution to this problem is to use CBU as a substrate **(3–22)**. If this, however, is not possible, then it's best to use water-resistant plywood, for

example, marine or exterior-grade plywood.

Marine plywood is a good choice for damp locations because it is waterproof and smooth with all holes and defects filled in. It is, however, very expensive and using it can put a serious dent in the budget. Another possibility is AC exterior-grade plywood. It is essential to carefully examine each sheet of exterior-grade plywood before buying. Many pieces are warped, have unfilled cavities, or have separations between the plies. Some sheets may also have beads of wood rosin on the surface. Rosin beads are undesirable because they can prevent the tile adhesive from adhering to the surface of the wood.

Concrete and Mortar Beds
Generally, concrete slabs provide an excellent substrate provided the surface is level and flat. Also, concrete prepared with liquid curing

compounds (called admixture) may resist the tile adhesive, preventing a good bond. It may also be difficult to achieve a good bond if the concrete has a smooth troweled finish.

It is not easy to pour a concrete slab so it forms the ideal surface for tiling; therefore, most concrete surfaces need additional preparation, leveling, and waterproofing before installing the tile.

Mortar, or mud, beds are the traditional surfaces for tiles preferred by most tilers. Many tile installers consider the mud bed the most desirable type of substrate because it remains dimensionally stable even during temperature and humidity fluctuations.

The main problem with a good mud bed is that it can raise the level of the floor by as much as two inches. This is not a problem in a new house because the builder is usually aware of the problem and plans the surrounding floor surfaces accordingly, but it can be a concern in a remodeling job.

A traditional mortar bed is composed of a 50/50 mixture of portland cement and fine sand. Fine sand is essential to this mix because it has no pebbles to cause bumps in the final surface. (It is important to note that while all sand may look alike, there are significant differences. Aggregate sand for a concrete mix is made from crushed stone. It combines with the concrete to form a strong bond. It also reduces the amount of shrinkage that would eventually cause cracking in the final surface. Beach sand does not combine as well with concrete and should never be used for aggregate.) The cement is mixed to a paste consistency, and then poured or shoveled onto the floor. It is then smoothed and screeded to create a level surface. Laying down a good mortar substrate and leveling it properly requires considerable skill and experience **(3–23)**.

Recently a variation on the traditional cement mix was introduced. It is called "drypack" and, though it is composed of portland cement and sand, it does not require as much water. The drypack is mixed to the consistency of wet sand and then shoveled onto the floor. The smoothing operation is the same as for the traditional cement mix.

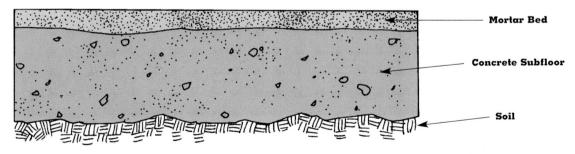

3–23. *Concrete slabs are strong and stable, but the surface is not always even or level. One way to level a concrete slab and smooth out irregularities in the surface is by adding a one- to two-inch layer of mortar. The mortar bed must be screeded and smoothed to make sure that the surface is perfectly flat.*

4–1. *A bathroom tile installation is considered to be an area where the water from the tub and shower can add a significant amount of humidity to the atmosphere. While a tiled surface may seem waterproof, it is not. Therefore, it is essential to install a water-resistant substrate, and even a waterproof membrane to the walls and floor to protect the framing from the possible effects of water damage.*

Installing the Substrate

Tile installations can add a considerable amount of weight to any structure. If a house or room is presently under construction, the builder should be aware that specific areas will receive tile installations. Walls and floors that are constructed accurately in the initial stages of construction will be easier to tile and will save the installer many headaches later on.

The American National Standards Institute publishes a book that outlines the structural requirements for any wall or floor that will be tiled. Included are specifications for strength and requirements for plumb, level, and flat surfaces. Obviously, the builder should have a copy of the ANSI specifica-

tions. Another useful manual that outlines installation requirements is the *Handbook for Ceramic Tile Installation*, published by the Tile Council of America.

Older houses must be carefully inspected to make sure that all support members are strong enough to carry the additional weight of the tile. It may be helpful to have an architect or engineer inspect the house before going too far into the tile job.

When the structural integrity of the supports is certain, proceed to the next part of the job—checking the floors and walls to be sure that they are flat, level, and plumb. This is important because a tile installation, even with plain tiles, has a prominent pattern

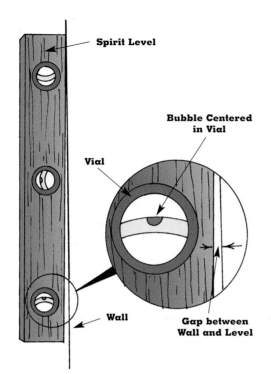

Spirit Level

Bubble Centered in Vial

Vial

Wall

Gap between Wall and Level

4–2. A spirit level can also be used to check the plumb of a wall, although it is a little more difficult than using a plumb bob. Hold the level against the wall and move it until the bubble in the vial shows that the instrument is level. Use a ruler to measure any gaps between the level and the wall. A deviation of over $^{1}/_{8}$ inch over a length of 8 feet is acceptable.

throughout. Deviations in the wall or floor surface will skew the tile alignment, resulting in an unsightly job.

A ruler, level, plumb bob, straightedges, and a length of cord are the only tools needed to make these checks. Start with the walls. Hang the plumb bob from the top and use a ruler to measure the distance between the wall and bob cord. A deviation of $^{1}/_{8}$ inch over a length of 8 feet or less is acceptable; greater variances must be corrected before attempting to install the tile. In lieu of a

plumb bob, a long spirit level can also be used to check wall plumb, but it is a more difficult way to measure deviations from the true vertical (**4–2**).

When checking the plumb, make numerous—not just one—checks along the entire length of the wall. It is not uncommon for a wall to be straight at one end and warped at the other. Also make sure that adjacent walls are plumb to each other.

After the walls, inspect the floor with the spirit level (**4–3**). Deviations of $^{1}/_{8}$ inch for 10 feet or less are acceptable, but greater discrepancies can affect the appearance of the final installation.

Since most rooms are rectangles, the corners where walls meet or where the floor joins the walls should form as right angles, that is, they should be square. If the corners are not square, proper tile alignment will have to be accomplished by cutting the perimeter tiles (the tiles around the edge of the field tiles) to fit the angled areas. A carpenter's square will indicate whether the corners are accurate or not (**4–4**), but since the tool is only 24 inches long, this may not be accurate for the whole wall.

For an inside corner, the Pythagorean theorem[1] can be used to check for square (**4–5**). Mark off a length of 3 feet along one wall, and 4 feet along the adjacent wall. Stretch a diagonal cord across the walls from one mark to the other. In effect, one wall is the base of a triangle, the other wall the height, and the cord becomes the hypotenuse (the side of a right-angled triangle that is opposite the right angle). If the cord measures

---

1. The Pythagorean theorem postulates that the square of the length of the hypotenuse of a right triangle equals the sum of the squares of the lengths of the other two sides.

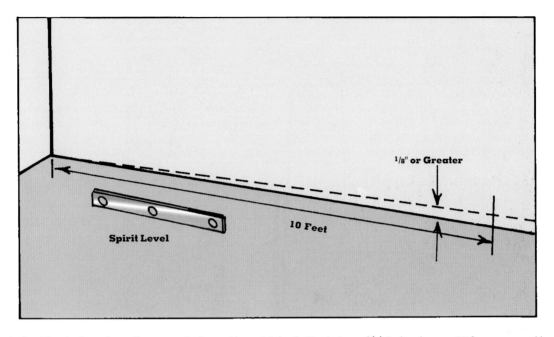

4–3. *After checking the walls, inspect the floor with a spirit level. Deviations of ¹/₈ inch or less per 10 feet are acceptable.*

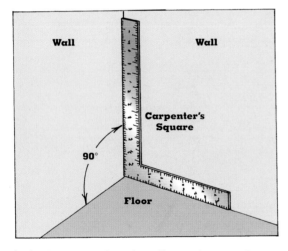

4–4. *The corners where the walls meet form at right angles, i.e., 90 degrees. Use a carpenter's square to check this angle.*

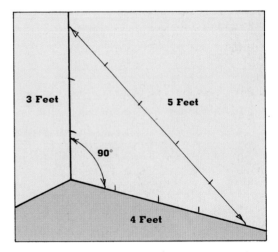

4–5. *The Pythagorean theorem can also be used to check the wall angles. Mark off a length of 3 feet along one wall and 4 feet along an adjacent wall. Stretch a diagonal cord across the wall from one mark to the other. In effect, one wall is the base of the triangle, the other wall is the height, and the cord becomes the hypotenuse. If the cord measures 5 feet, then the walls form a perfect right angle and are square. For longer walls, 6-8-10 or 9-12-15 feet can be substituted to create the right angle.*

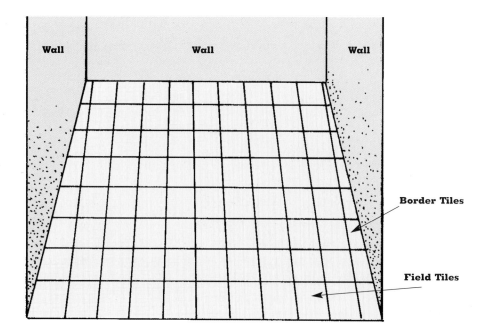

4–6. *In rooms where the floor or wall angles are irregular and out of square, it may be necessary to draw a layout grid on the surface to be tiled. This will help you to decide where the field tiles should be placed and which border tiles may have to be cut.*

exactly 5 feet, then the walls form a perfect right triangle and are square. For longer walls, 6-8-10 feet or 9-12-25 feet can be substituted to create the right triangle.

If the walls are seriously out of square, they must be rebuilt or else extra care must be taken to plan the installation. This means laying down a square set of reference lines to align the tiles **(4–6)**.

INSTALLING CEMENT BACKER BOARDS

Cement backer boards (CBUs) are the preferred substrate for most tile installations. Cutting and mounting the boards are within the skills of most do-it-yourselfers and only a few basic tools are needed.

The simplest way to cut the boards is with a carbide-tipped scriber. First, it's neces-

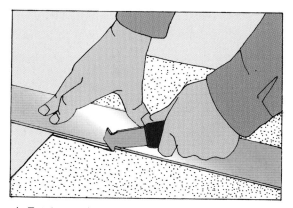

4–7. *The simplest way to cut cement backer board, also called cementitious backer unit (abbreviated CBU), is with a carbide-tipped scriber. Mark the cutting line accurately on both sides of the board. Using a straightedge as a guide, draw the scriber along the mark several times. The scriber should cut through the fiberglass mesh and make a deep groove into the board.*

sary to mark the cutting line accurately on both sides of the board **(4–7)**. Use a straightedge to guide the scriber. Lay the straightedge on the board and then draw the scriber along the mark several times. The scriber should cut through the strands of fiberglass mesh on the surface and make a deep groove into the board.

Unlike gypsum wallboard, which only needs to be scribed on one side, the backer board must be scored on both sides to make a clean break. When this is accomplished, hold one side of the board down while pulling up on the other. The board should snap into two pieces at the scored line **(4–8)**. The break will not be entirely smooth, but will have a rough core. This should be smoothed down with a masonry rubbing stone **(4–9)**.

A cleaner cut can be made with a diamond saw in a hand grinder **(4–10)**. Here again, it's best to attempt the cut by making several shallow passes on each side. The first pass should only be deep enough to cut through the fiberglass mesh on the surface.

4–8. *To make the break, press down on one side of the board and pull up on the other.*

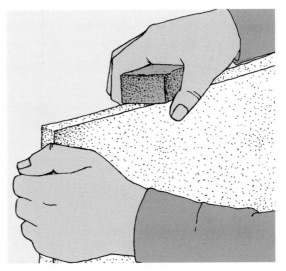

4–9. *The edges along the break will be rough. These can be smoothed with a masonry rubbing stone.*

4–10. *A cleaner cut can be made with a diamond saw fitted in a hand grinder. It is best to make the cut by making several shallow passes on each side. The first pass should only be deep enough to cut through the fiberglass mesh on the surface. Attempting to make a deeper cut will only tear the mesh and damage its reinforcing value.*

4–11. *In addition to making straight cuts, it may be necessary to drill holes for fixtures and pipes. These holes can be cut with a carbide-tipped hole saw chucked into an electric drill. It's best to start the hole from one side, cutting halfway through the board. Then turn the board over and complete the hole from the other side.*

Attempting to make a deeper cut with the initial pass will only tear the mesh and damage its reinforcing value. In most cases, the final cut will be smooth, but occasionally the board may snap prematurely, and it will be necessary to dress the edge with the rubbing stone.

A hand grinder produces large quantities of dust that can be harmful to inhale. If possible, do this kind of cutting outdoors, and wear a respirator specified by the National Institute of Occupational Safety and Health (NIOSH).

In addition to making straight cuts, it will sometimes be necessary to cut holes for plumbing fixtures and pipes. Small holes of an inch or two in diameter can be cut with a carbide-tipped hole saw. It's best to cut the hole halfway from one side **(4–11)**, and then turn the board over and complete the hole from the other.

Larger holes can be made by first outlining the hole on the board and then drilling a series of small holes within the outline using an electric drill fitted with a carbide-tipped bit. Use the hand scriber to cut through the mesh on both sides, and then tap out the hole with a hammer. Smooth the edges of the hole with an abrasive stone or a rasp.

The best way to mount backer boards to a vertical surface is with screws made specifically for CBUs. These screws have a corrosion-resistant coating and are designed to countersink so that the heads will be flush with the surface of the board when they are installed. The boards should be mounted so that the screws bite directly into the underlying studs. For maximum support, the edges of the boards should rest directly on studs. This may mean adding additional studs to the framing if a board ends between existing studs.

Start the screws by tapping them with a

hammer, and then use an electric screwdriver or drill fitted with a screwdriver bit to drive the screws home. The screws should be spaced 6 and 8 inches apart. Use $1^1/4$-inch screws to mount the board directly to the studs, and 2-inch screws to mount the board over a layer of drywall.

Occasionally a screw may break as it is being driven into the board. If part of the screw projects above the surface, remove it by gripping the shaft with a pair of pliers and twisting it out. Under no circumstances should it be driven in further with a hammer. This could damage the surrounding backer board. If the screw is flush or below the surface, leave it and drive another one about one 1 inch away.

Since backer board is susceptible to expansion, it will be necessary to leave a $1/8$-inch gap between the boards to allow for movement between them. If the backer board surrounds a tub or shower, leave a larger expansion gap of $1/4$ inch. This gap can later be filled with flexible sealant.

Mounting backer board (CBU) to a horizontal surface, for example, wooden subflooring, requires the same techniques as vertical installations; however, a layer of thinset mortar should be applied to the subfloor surface before laying down the backer board. The best mortar to use is one that is made expressly for mounting CBUs, usually a latex- or acrylic-modified thinset adhesive.

Manufacturers' instructions may vary somewhat, depending upon the product, so it is important for the installer to read the manufacturer's directions carefully before spreading the adhesive. Always, however, the initial step is to thoroughly clean the subfloor before applying the adhesive. The surface should be carefully vacuumed to remove any loose dust, and then damp-mopped to remove heavier dirt and grit.

Since the backer board will be secured to the underlying joists, it is important to locate them and mark their positions on the subfloor. Whenever possible, the backer boards should be cut and placed so their edges terminate over a joist; otherwise, it will be necessary to add additional bracing to the framing below the floor. The cutting operation should be done in another area, so cutting dust does not contaminate the freshly cleaned substrate surface.

The adhesive can be applied with a steel trowel, but it must be forced into the contours of the subflooring to ensure a good bond. Spread the thinset with the straight side of the trowel, by holding the tool at a sharp angle—about 10 to 20 degrees—and pressing down hard. When an even, thick coat of adhesive has been spread, turn the trowel over to the notched side and run it through the coat. Hold the trowel at a wider angle—45 to 70 degrees—to comb through the adhesive and build up a series of uniform ridges.

Tip the CBU onto the adhesive while is still wet and tacky, and then press down hard to make sure it seats properly. Continue this procedure until the entire subfloor is covered; remember, however, to leave $1/8$-inch expansion joints between sheets of CBU and $1/4$-inch joints between the board and surrounding walls. (Expansion joints are discussed in the next chapter.)

There are two schools of thought concerning how to proceed from this point. Some installers feel that no other preparation

4–12. *After mounting the boards on the wall, cover all the joints with fiberglass mesh tape.*

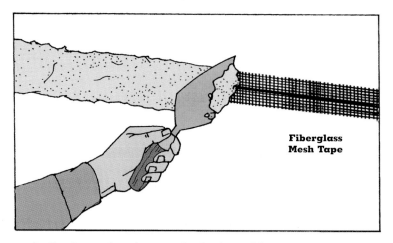

Fiberglass Mesh Tape

4–13. *After pressing the fiberglass mesh in place, trowel a thin layer of thinset mortar (use the same adhesive that will be used to set the tiles) over the mesh. Smooth the mortar and feather the edges to create a flat surface.*

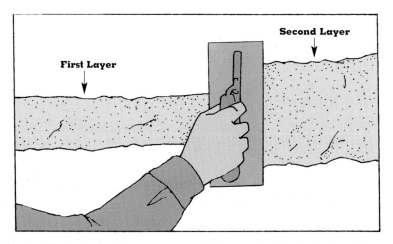

Second Layer

First Layer

4–14. *After the adhesive has had time to set, a second layer can be added to the first. Use a wide trowel to smooth and feather the edges.*

is needed and tile-setting may commence. Other installers feel that all the joints should be sealed and taped to add additional strength and moisture resistance to the surface. Certainly taping is relatively inexpensive and, since it requires only a small amount of additional time and expense, it is probably well worth doing.

Cover the joints with adhesive-backed, fiberglass-mesh tape made for CBUs **(4–12)**, and then trowel a thin layer of thinset mortar over it (use the same mortar that will be used to lay the tiles) **(4–13)**. Feather and flatten the edges to create a smooth surface **(4–14)**.

INSTALLING DRYWALL

Drywall is not moisture-resistant like cement backer boards, but it can be an acceptable substrate in dry areas. It can also be waterproofed to serve in light-duty wet areas. It is installed much the same way as CBUs,

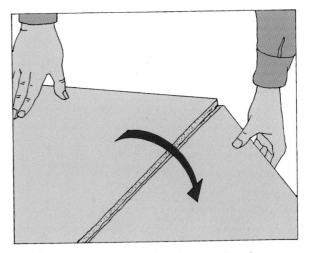

4–16. *Bend the board away from the score. Turn the board over and press down on one side while holding the other side securely. This will cause it to break evenly at the score line.*

although it is easier to cut and fasten in place.

To cut drywall, use a utility knife to score through the paper surface into the core of the board **(4–15)**. Use a straightedge to ensure a straight cut. Bending the board away from the

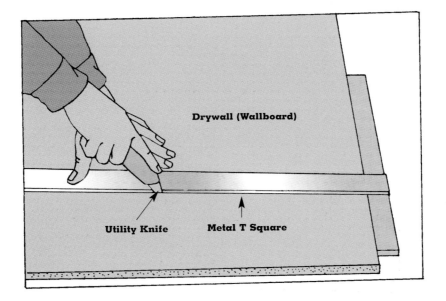

Drywall (Wallboard)

Utility Knife   Metal T Square

4–15. *To cut drywall, use a sharp utility knife to score through the surfacing paper into the core of the plaster. Use a straightedge as a guide for accuracy.*

4–17. *Fold the board back and cut the paper on the opposite side.*

scored surface will cause it to snap and break on the scored line **(4–16)**. Fold the board back and cut the paper on the opposite side of the break by running the utility knife through the crease **(4–17)**. Smooth the edges of the cut with a piece of coarse sandpaper wrapped around a block.

Use ringed nails or wallboard screws to mount the drywall in place. Make sure that the fasteners penetrate through the board into a stud.

Do not use standard drywall tape to cover the joints between the boards. It has a paper base that isn't waterproof; nor is it strong enough to support the tiles. Instead, use an open-weave, fiberglass-mesh tape. Fiberglass-mesh tape is available with, and without, self-adhesive backing. Obviously, the self-adhesive tape is easier to install because it can simply be pressed in place. The nonadhesive tape must be stapled.

In areas where there is already a drywall covering, it may be advantageous to add another layer. The second layer can provide additional strength and rigidity to the existing wall, thereby creating a solid substrate for the tile; it can hide any defects or flaws in the existing surface.

INSTALLING PLYWOOD

Plywood does not make an ideal substrate because it absorbs moisture readily and it flexes under weight. Still, there are times that, for reasons of cost or availability, it may be the only choice. To be a stable substrate, it must be at least $1\frac{1}{8}$ inches thick. Rather than attempting to install a layer of plywood this thick, it is far better to create the thickness with two layers. A double layer provides the additional benefit of being firmer and more rigid than a single thick layer. Thus, a layer of $\frac{1}{2}$-inch-thick plywood can be laminated to an underlying layer of $\frac{5}{8}$-inch plywood to achieve the necessary thickness.

Plywood can, of course, be cut with ordinary hand or power tools designed for wood-

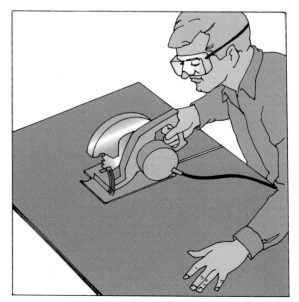

4–18. *Use a power saw to cut plywood.*

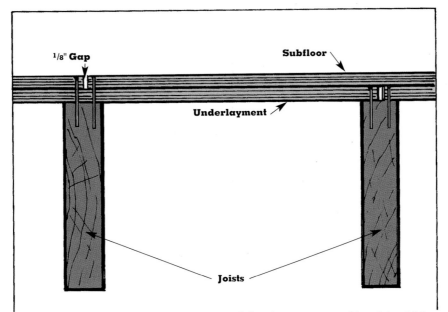

4–19. *When laying down plywood, position the panels so all the edges are supported by a joist. Make sure that the joints of the subfloor do not coincide with those of the underlayment. Joints between the panels should have a $^1/_8$-inch gap for expansion. These can be filled with tile-setting adhesive.*

working or carpentry **(4–18)**. The sheets can be secured with flat-head screws or ring-shank nails. These fasteners should be positioned a minimum of 6 inches apart and should penetrate through both layers of plywood into the joists below or studs behind. Ideally, their length should be about three times the thickness of the plywood. All nail or screw heads should be sunk below the surface of the floor; otherwise, tiles resting on the protruding heads can crack or break when subjected to weight.

Before installing the top layer, for example the subfloor, or plywood, on the plywood underlayment, spread a layer of construction adhesive rated for floor use. Most plywood sheets have two surfaces—one coarse, the other a little smoother. The coarse side

should face up; this will give the tile adhesive some "tooth" (a rough or textured surface) and ensure a tighter bond.

Position the panels so all edges are supported by a joist, and so the joints of the subfloor layer do not coincide with those of the underlayment **(4–19)**. Joints between the panels should have a gap for expansion of $^1/_8$ inch. These can be later be filled with tile-setting adhesive.

When both layers are installed, carefully inspect the surface for damaged wood fibers that may be sticking up. These can be smoothed with sandpaper.

All that remains to prepare the subfloor for the tile installation is to clean the surface and remove all dust with a vacuum.

5

CHAPTER

Expansion Joints and Moisture Barriers

EXPANSION JOINTS

The theory behind using expansion joints has to do with the concept that fluctuations in temperatures and the rise of humidity—even at rates that are almost imperceptible to our senses—cause building materials to expand and contract as they absorb and release heat and moisture. The amount of expansion or contraction depends

5–1. *Should a mositure barrier or waterproof membrane be installed or not? This is an important question that should be addressed when installing tile in a wet area, such as a bathroom. Cement and cement backer board are water-resistant but not waterproof. A waterproof membrane can offer extra protection, particularly to the tiled divider between the tub and lavatory, from excess water.*

upon not only the amount of heat and moisture in the air, but also the nature of the building materials. Dissimilar materials will move at different rates **(5–2).**

These changes in structural dimensions could cause materials or surfaces to buckle and crack if builders did not introduce some control mechanism to allow the materials to move. The control mechanism is a simple gap filled with flexible materials such as foam and resilient caulk or sealant.

Not everyone agrees on the need for expansion joints, the best width, or the materials to fill them. Some installers insist on a gap of at least $1/4$ inch around large floors and around all plumbing fixtures, while others

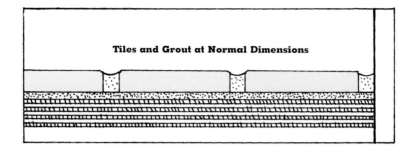

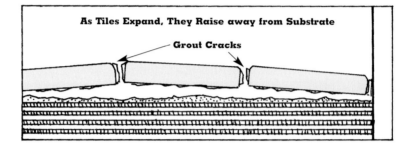

5–2. *Dissimilar materials will expand at different rates as temperature and humidity fluctuate. In extreme conditions, the tile surface may lift off the substrate and crack.*

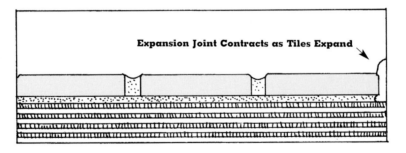

5–3. *A flexible expansion joint around the perimeter of the tile bed will absorb the expansion and prevent it from lifting off and cracking.*

feel that ¹/₈ inch is sufficient. They also believe that these gaps should be filled with flexible caulk; ordinary grout is too rigid and using it as a filler defeats the purpose of an expansion joint.

Other installers eliminate the expansion joint. They feel that the average bathroom or kitchen floor is small enough to remain dimensionally stable and there really is no need for any expansion joint. In most cases, they are right. Temperature and humidity in most homes is relatively stable—even in moist rooms like the bathroom—so the tiles do not really flex; and the substructure is more or less isolated from ambient fluctuations, making expansion joints equally unnecessary. Furthermore, as those who oppose using expansion joints are quick to point out, flexible caulk is not as durable as grout and it often detracts from the final appearance of the job.

Installers who favor expansion joints will construct a network of joints in tile fields of very large commercial surfaces, but for most home installations they settle for an expansion joint around the perimeter of the floor (5–3). They feel, however, that all floors laid over a substrate of two different materials, such as cement backer board and plywood, should have an additional expansion joint over the seam where these two substrates meet. Indeed, in this situation, most authorities favor an expansion joint. Fortunately, most homes do not have substrates bridged with dissimilar materials.

In addition to perimeter joints, it is also necessary to isolate the floor from any pipes that may penetrate through the floor. Metal pipes will expand at a greater rate than the floor tiles—this is particularly true of hot-water pipes—so they will exert pressure against the tiles as they expand, unless they are isolated with an expansion gap. Likewise, tiles mounted on walls should also have gaps around the pipes coming through the wall surface. All tile installers cut oversized holes to accommodate the pipes coming through the walls. In most cases, they are not as concerned with expansion; they simply find it easier to fit the tiles around the pipes if they cut a large hole. They cover the hole with an escutcheon plate.

All installers leave a gap between the wall tiles and the bathtub that they fill with a flexible caulk. The reason for this has less to do with the different rates of expansion between the tub and surrounding walls than with the need for additional waterproofing around the perimeter of the tub. This area is prone to water accumulations that could quickly penetrate ordinary grout and cause it to disintegrate. Flexible caulk is a better choice for this joint.

On countertops, there should be an expansion joint between the tiles and sink, and between the surface, or deck tiles, and the backsplash. Here again, waterproofing is probably as important as expansion.

If you decide to include expansion joints, you'll find that they are easy to make and fill. It is only necessary to leave a $1/4$-inch gap between the dissimilar materials. If the gap extends to the tile level, and not into the substrate, as, for example, in a countertop installation, it is only necessary to fill it with caulking. For deeper gaps, it is a good idea to push a foam backer rod into the joint before caulking. Foam backer rod is essentially a flexible and compressible dowel of polyurethane foam. It is not, strictly speaking, a tile-related product and therefore may not be available in tile supply stores. It will, however, be available at hardware stores or home centers wherever caulking is sold.

CAULKS

There are different types of caulk on the market. Silicone-based and polysulfide caulks are used by many professionals because they remain flexible for many years and are therefore more durable. They tend to be very sticky and are, therefore, difficult to apply and clean up. In addition, they are only available in a limited range of colors, so they may not match every color scheme.

Urethane caulks are a better choice for most jobs. They are available in a wide range of colors and offer the convenience of easy cleanup. Whatever brand or type of caulk that's used, always read the manufacturer's instructions regarding application specifics such as temperature and humidity limitations and curing requirements.

Some caulks are available in flexible tubes, similar to toothpaste but with a longer nozzle, that must be squeezed to force out the contents. These may be cheaper than the cartridges if only a small amount of caulk is needed, but it is difficult to maintain steady hand pressure, so the bead will not be even or consistent.

Cartridges are a better choice for most jobs. Almost all flexible caulks are available in cartridges that will drop into standard caulking guns. Applying the caulk is fairly easy. First, cut the tip off the cartridge nozzle. The nozzle is tapered, and this feature makes it possible to shape the width of the bead. Cutting close to the tip creates a narrow bead, while a higher cut will make a wider bead. There may be a foil seal inside the nozzle. Puncture this with a sharp nail or stiff wire.

To load the caulking gun, rotate the plunger rod so that the notches face up and then pull it all the way back. Drop the cartridge into the gun and reverse the rod. Squeeze the trigger enough to bring the plunger into contact with the cartridge, but not enough to force the caulk out.

Before applying a bead of caulk to any joint, clean it by removing any dirt or debris.

There are two basic beading techniques: the "push" method and the "pull" method. To push a bead, hold the gun at a 60-degree angle and start squeezing the trigger **(5–4)**. As the caulk emerges, move the gun forward. The bead will be formed behind the gun. This method tends to push more caulk into the crack, but it makes an uneven bead.

The pull method is exactly the opposite **(5–5)**. Hold the gun at a lower angle—45 degrees—and squeeze the trigger. Pull the gun back as the bead forms. This method tends to stretch the bead out, making it thinner but smoother.

After the bead is drawn, smooth it with your index finger. If a sticky caulk is being used, it may help to coat your finger with a lubricant like soapy water to prevent the caulk from sticking to your skin. When the joint is relatively smooth, remove the excess caulk with a damp sponge. It's best to make several light passes with the sponge rather than one heavy-handed one. This will remove the excess surface material without pulling caulk out of the joint.

WATERPROOF MEMBRANES

If the concept of expansion joints is cause for debate, the topic of waterproof membranes (moisture barriers) is only slightly less so. A waterproof membrane is an impervious barrier that keeps moisture from penetrating behind the tiles to the vulnerable framing in the walls.

Many people assume that if the walls are of cement, cement backer board, or moisture-resistant wallboard, there is no need for a waterproof membrane. And in some cases, they are right. Whether a waterproof membrane should be installed depends upon the environment, that is, wet or dry. For example, a family-room floor would be considered a dry environment.

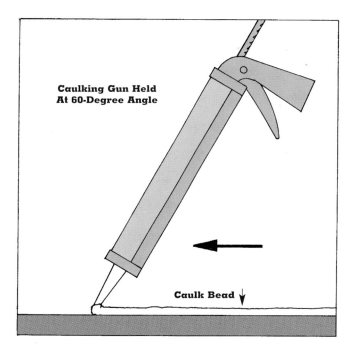

5–4. *To "push" a caulk bead, hold the caulking gun at a 60-degree angle, squeeze the trigger, and slowly push the bead away from you.*

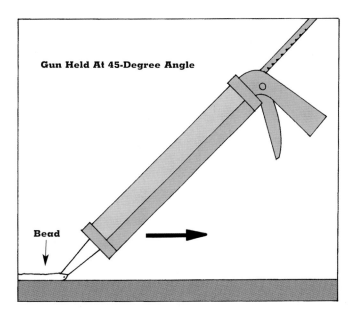

5–5. *To "pull" a caulk bead, hold the caulking gun at a lower, 45-degree angle, squeeze the trigger, and slowly pull the bead toward you.*

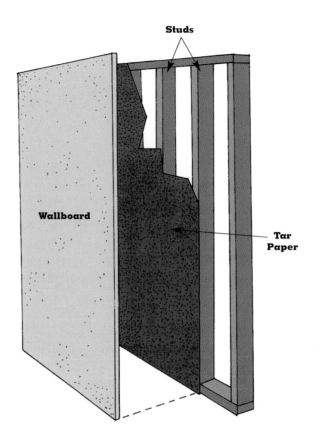

Studs

Wallboard

Tar
Paper

5–6. *Tar paper or building felt stapled to the framing studs can be an effective moisture barrier. The paper must be installed before the wallboard is put into place. Obviously, this is best done while the house is under construction or during an extensive remodeling project.*

Defining a wet environment becomes a little more problematic. For example, a bathroom may be considered a dry environment if it has only a sink and a toilet, or if there is only a bathtub and not a shower. The inclusion of a shower changes that bathroom into a wet environment, and here it is best to install a waterproof membrane. Still, some people balk at adding a waterproof membrane to shower walls for a number of reasons, the added cost being the primary one.

In some cases, the decision to install the waterproof membrane may not always be an option for either the builder or the home owner. Often, building codes specifically require these membranes in certain areas, and disregarding the codes can have serious legal consequences.

There are different types of membrane. The simplest is ordinary building felt or tar paper. This can be stapled to the studs before the backer board or wallboard is put up **(5–6)**. Obviously, this must be installed as the house is being built or during an extensive remodeling project that exposes the framing.

Tar paper is an effective barrier that can safeguard the studs but offers absolutely no protection for the surfacing material on top, for example the wallboard. Gypsum wallboard is not waterproof and requires an additional membrane to keep moisture out. At this point a question arises: If the wallboard has a surface membrane that blocks all moisture, why use the tar paper at all? Indeed, it is a cogent point. Only a few installers or builders who like to be on the safe side put tar paper up; the majority of installers dispense with it entirely.

While membranes offer solid protection against moisture penetration, many installers feel that adequate waterproofing can be achieved by adding waterproofing to the thinset mix (this is not possible with pre-mixed mastics). The thinset then becomes an adhesive and a waterproof membrane.

This technique is fine for most home areas (including showers and baths) that receive average use, provided the substrate is backer board and not ordinary drywall. In high-moisture areas, like steam rooms, water will eventually seep through and damage the substrate and framing.

For these installations, it's best to install a waterproof membrane. Membranes are made of plastic sheathing, such as sheathing made with chlorinated polyethylene, laminated to a high-strength, nonwoven fabric. They are about .030 inch (0.8 mm) thick and are available in 100-foot rolls that are 5 feet wide. One roll will cover about 500 square feet. Surfaces wider than 5 feet can be covered by overlapping sheets. They should overlap by at least 2 inches and be bonded with solvent specified by the manufacturer.

Depending upon the product and manufacturer's recommendations, the membrane may be applied on a layer of acrylic or polymeric modified thinset, or special adhesives created by the manufacturer. Even though the membrane is flexible, it should only be installed on a flat surface. Surfaces with depressions may cause the membrane to bridge over the gap, leaving air bubbles.

After the membrane is laid down, it's best to flatten and press it into the adhesive with a heavy roller. Most membranes do not require any curing time (check manufacturer's recommendations), so that the tiles may be laid down immediately after they are in place.

6

CHAPTER

Setting the Tiles

MIXING AND APPLYING THINSET ADHESIVE

There are a number of ready-to-use adhesives that require no mixing, but most tile setters find that site-mixed thinset adhesives offer more in terms of performance, workability, and permanence. They are not difficult to mix, but it is important to read the manufacturer's specifications and instructions carefully. In most cases, these will include the ratios of liquid to mortar, and also recommendations for spreading trowels.

Most thinset products are not toxic, but mixing the powder can often raise quantities of dust, so it's a good idea to wear a dust mask and make sure the working area is well ventilated. The thinset can be hard on bare skin because it absorbs moisture, so wear rubber gloves and keep a pail of water nearby so you can wash any thinset off your arms or hands.

Start by bringing all the ingredients to

6–1 (opposite page). *A striking floor pattern that uses large pavers with smaller pieces at corner points. Like all tile installations, this one required care when setting the tiles to ensure a quality job.* **(Photo courtesy of Dal-Til Company)**

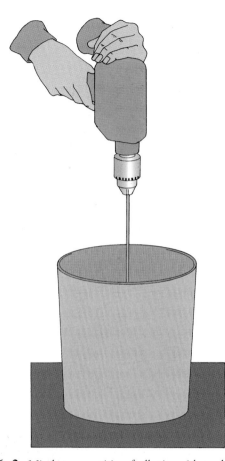

6–2. *Mix large quantities of adhesive with an electric drill and a mixing paddle. Use a paddle designed for this, not a paint-mixing attachment. The drill speed should not exceed 300 rpm or the paddle will create air bubbles in the mixture. This could disperse the adhesive and weaken its bonding power.*

the work site so they have time to adjust to the temperature and humidity of the area. The room temperature should be maintained at 50⁰ F to 70⁰ F for at least 24 hours prior to installation. For mixes that require water, use only clean drinking water that is free of impurities. Mix all the ingredients in clean, dry containers.

Start by pouring the liquid into the mixing bucket and then slowly adding the powder. For small quantities, a hand trowel is an adequate mixing tool. For larger quantities, a mixing paddle (use a paddle designed for mortar mixing, not paint mixing) can be chucked into an electric drill **(6–2)**. Be sure, however, that the drill speed does not exceed 300 rpm or else the paddle will create air bubbles in the mixture and disperse the adhesive.

Once the thinset is mixed, allow it to stand for 10 minutes. This waiting period is called "slaking"; it allows the dry particles in the mix to fully absorb all the liquid. After the slaking, remix the adhesive.

Mixing Epoxy Thinsets

The technique for mixing epoxy thinsets is similar to that for regular thinsets except that greater care must be taken to get the proportions exactly right. For some products, the amount of hardener will equal the amount of resin. With other products, the amounts will vary, so it is essential to read the manufacturer's directions carefully before starting.

Since the combination of hardener and resin will generate heat, it is best to mix these ingredients together by hand. Using an electric drill and paddle could introduce more heat into the mixture, causing it to harden prematurely.

Spreading the Adhesive

The ideal ambient temperature for spreading the adhesives is between 65⁰ F and 75⁰ F. If the temperature drops below 50⁰ F, it could retard the curing time of the adhesive or even, in extreme cases, cause it to freeze up. If the temperature rises, it will accelerate the drying time and make the adhesive unworkable.

Before spreading the adhesive, it is a good idea to test it to make sure it is of the right consistency. If the adhesive is too wet, it cannot be combed into ridges; if it is too dry, it will not adhere to the tiles. An easy way to test the consistency is by piling a glob on the trowel and then inverting it. If the adhesive runs, it is too wet. If it drops off the trowel, it is too dry. If it remains and retains its shape, it is the right consistency and can be spread.

The adhesive is first spread on the substrate with the straight or "unnotched" side of the trowel (6–3). The trowel should be held at an acute angle of about 30 degrees. The object here is to cover a workable area and force the adhesive into the cracks and pores of the substrate. If guidelines have been set up for the tile placement, be sure that the adhesive doesn't cover or obliterate them.

After the adhesive has been spread, it is combed with the notched side of the trowel (6–4). Adhesive trowels have different tooth profiles and sizes. Choosing the right tooth size and shape is largely determined by the tile to be installed. For example, use a V-notch with teeth $5/32$ inch wide and deep for installing ceramic mosaics. For installing standard wall tiles, flat-back ceramic tiles, or quarry and vitreous tiles, use a square-notch trowel with $1/4$-inch teeth. For larger tiles or for slate and marble tiles, it is better to use a square-notch trowel with $3/8$-inch-deep teeth. When combing the adhesive, hold the trowel at a wider angle, about 45 degrees, so the trowel teeth penetrate fully into the mixture.

Spreading the right amount of adhesive is a concern for novice tile setters. If too much is spread, it may start to dry and "skin" over before the tiles can be set properly. In this case, the bond will not be secure and eventually the tiles may pop up. It's best, then, to

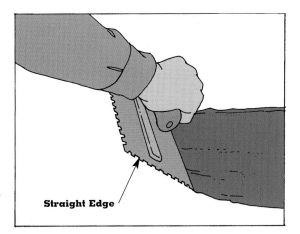

6–3. *Spread the adhesive on the substrate with the unnotched side of the trowel. Spread the adhesive by holding the trowel at an angle of about 30 degrees and at the same time force the adhesive into the cracks and pores of the substrate.*

6–4. *After spreading the adhesive, turn the trowel around and use the notched side to comb the adhesive layer.*

spread only a small amount of adhesive, say about a square yard, and see how long it takes to set the tiles in that area. If you find that you can work quickly and accurately enough, continue by spreading a larger area.

Another factor to take into consideration when spreading the adhesive is the ambient temperature of the working environment. If the room is warm, the adhesive will dry faster;

so it may not be practical to spread too much or else it will skin over before the tiles can be set.

SETTING THE TILES

Once the adhesive is spread, start placing the tiles. This is an easy operation requiring little skill; it is important, however, to make sure that each tile aligns properly with its neighbor. Use the straightedge and level often to check the accuracy of the work. Take the first tile, position it in place (aligning it to the guidelines or batten in the adhesive bed) and press down on it with your fingers.

Some tile setters like to twist the tile slightly as they press it into the adhesive; they feel it spreads the adhesive against the tile back and creates a firmer bond. In theory, this sounds like a good idea, and it may work for the first few tiles; but as more tiles are set against each other, it will become more difficult to twist them without disturbing the neighboring pieces. Another problem with this practice is that if the tiles are twisted too vigorously, they could push the adhesive up along the edges of the tile surface. This can also happen if the tiles are slid rather than pressed into place.

After pressing the first tile in place, you can, if desired, pull it up again to see how much adhesive has spread across the back of the tile. Another way to gauge the consistency of the adhesive is to check the tile's entire surface; if the entire surface is evenly coated, then the consistency is good—provided that the adhesive hasn't oozed up along the sides of the tile. If it has, it usually indicates that the ridges in the combed adhesive are too wide. To correct the problem, recomb it with another trowel that has smaller teeth. If the

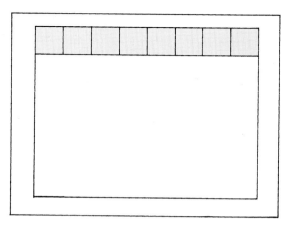

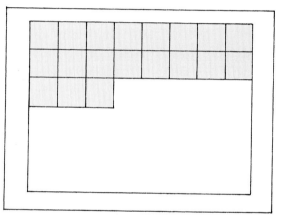

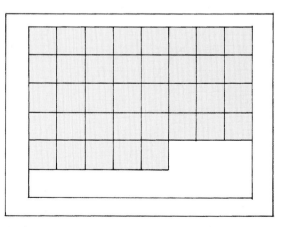

6–5 to 6–7. *One way to set field tiles is by laying down an entire row, laying the following row next to it, and following this with subsequent rows until the entire field is covered. If the first course is perfectly true, then the next courses with probably be straight as well. This method works well with small fields, but it can be difficult in large rooms or on fields that are not perfectly square.*

back of the tile has little or no adhesive adhering to it, the adhesive might be too dry or the comb may be too narrow. Try recombing it with a wide-toothed trowel before attempting to remix the adhesive.

There are two methods of laying a field of tiles. Some tile setters like to set an entire row, a course, before placing the neighboring tiles **(6–5 to 6–7)**. If this course is perfectly straight, then the rest of the field will probably be true also. This method works well in small rooms, but it can be awkward if a large field has to be covered. With the second method, a few feet of the first course are installed; then adjacent tiles are placed next to it, gradually forming a pyramid **(6–8 to 6–10)**. This method allows the installer to work in one area at a time and at the same time allows him to see the combined effect of the tile pattern as it takes shape. Choosing one or the other is largely a matter of personal preference.

In most cases, backbuttering will not be necessary, but occasionally a tile will sit lower than its neighbors. This may happen if there is a slight depression in the substrate, or if you are working with handmade tiles that are not of the same thickness. Backbuttering is simple, much like buttering a slice of bread (hence the name "buttering"). Hold the tile backside up and use a wide putty knife to spread some adhesive across the entire surface **(6–11)**. Bevel the adhesive around the edges of the tile so it doesn't push up into the joints as the tile is being placed. The adhesive's thickness is determined by the distance the tile will be raised to bring it level with the surrounding surface.

Whether or not it is better to install the

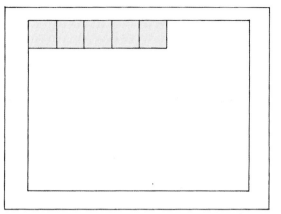

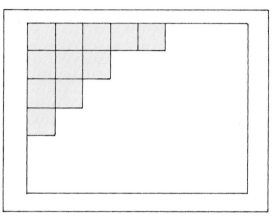

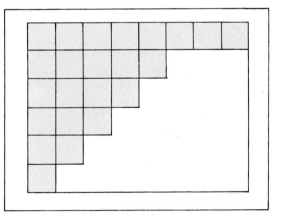

6–8 to 6–10. *With the pyramid method of laying tiles, a few feet of the first course are positioned, and then a few adjacent tiles are laid next to it. A few more tiles are added to the next row to gradually form a pyramid.*

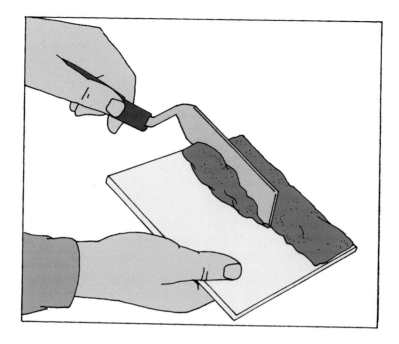

6–11. *To backbutter tile, hold the tile backside up and use a wide putty knife to spread some adhesive across the entire surface. Bevel the adhesive around the edges of the tile so it doesn't push up into the joints as you place the tile.*

border tiles (assuming that they have to be cut to fit in place) as the job progresses or wait until all the field tiles are in place is a more pressing concern. It takes time to cut tile. If the installation must be halted until a number of tiles are cut, then the adhesive could dry and skin over before they can be placed. In this case, it's better to concentrate on installing all the field tiles and then go back to do the border pieces. If, however, there is a helper who can cut the border tiles as you are laying down the others (as many professional tiles setters have), then they can be easily placed when the edges of the field are reached.

CLEANING UP EXCESS ADHESIVE

In most cases, if the adhesive was mixed properly and the tiles set carefully, the gaps between the tiles will be free of adhesive. In some places, however, the adhesive may have oozed up around the edges of the tile and filled the joints. This adhesive should be removed before installing the grout. If it is not removed, the grout layer will be thinner in these places than in the rest of the field. This can affect the final color of the grout—called "ghosting," the color will be noticeably lighter—and it will affect the strength of the grout.

For wide joints, a stick can be used if the adhesive is still soft. If it has hardened, use a small file to clean out the joints. In thinner joints, a grout saw or a utility knife can be used to work the adhesive out. Work carefully so the substrate isn't damaged; remember, the objective is to remove only the excess adhesive. To remove adhesive that may have set on the surface of the tiles, rub the tiles with a nonabrasive scouring pad (for example, a Scotch-Brite pad).

MIXING AND APPLYING THE GROUT

Applying the grout properly involves more than simply pushing it into the gaps between the tiles. Most tile setters are quick to point out that a good grouting job can often mask imperfections in the tile installation, while a poor grouting job can mar an otherwise outstanding tile installation.

Before applying any grout, consider the possible effect that it could have on the tiles. Most tiles are glazed or sealed so a layer of grout smoothed across their surface will have little or no effect on them. There are other tiles, however, particularly handmade ones, that are not sealed, and the grout could stain or discolor them.

It is best to test the tiles by smearing some grout on a spare tile. If there is no noticeable effect, proceed with the grouting. If the grout stains the tile, apply a removable sealer to the tiles before attempting to install the grout. Various types of sealer are available at tile supply stores. Consult with the dealer to determine which product is best for your needs.

The grouting job can be divided into four stages: mixing the grout, applying it, removing excess grout, and then cleaning and finishing the grouted joints. There are premixed grouts on the market; these are useful for filling in small gaps. It's better, however, to buy the powdered grout and mix it with liquid just prior to installation. This grout will be stronger and more durable than the premixed kind.

As with the adhesive, it's a good idea to bring all the grout ingredients into the work area a couple of hours before mixing them so they can adjust to the temperature and humidity conditions of the room. Depending upon the product, the grout can be either mixed with water (it should be clean and free of impurities) or a special liquid additive. Carefully read the instructions on the package to find out the exact amount of liquid to mix with the powder. It's best, however, to start with only two-thirds of that amount, because the powder may have absorbed moisture from the air, making the full quantity of liquid superfluous.

Pour the liquid into a clean, dry bucket. Slowly add the powder until the mixture becomes plastic and spreadable. If it becomes too thick, add more liquid. A hand trowel or a power mixing paddle chucked in an electric drill can be used for mixing the grout. If using the electric drill method, remember to keep the motor speed below 300 rpm.

It is important to get the right mix. Too much liquid will weaken the grout, while not enough will make it stiff and difficult to work. Properly mixed grout should be firm enough to hold peaks, yet plastic enough to be spreadable without running. After the grout is mixed, allow it stand or slake for about ten minutes. After the slaking, the mix may be slightly harder. If so, add a little more liquid, and then wait another ten minutes before applying the grout.

When the grout is properly mixed, it can be applied to the joints. Ideally, it should be applied when the ambient temperature is between 65° F and 75° F. Grout can be applied directly around vitreous tile, but for

6–12. *Spread the grout with a grout trowel. It has a rubber face that protects the tile surfaces. Hold the trowel at a low, 30-degree angle and push the grout across the tiles, forcing it into the gaps between the tiles. It is important to pack the grout and eliminate all voids.*

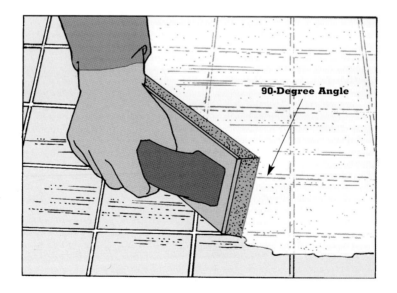

6–13. *After the gaps are filled with grout, reposition the trowel angle so that the blade is almost vertical. Work the trowel across the face of the tiles to scrape away any excess grout. Be sure not to gouge grout out of the gaps with the corners of the trowel.*

nonvitreous tile, it's a good idea to dampen the surface and edges of the tiles with a sponge before applying the grout. This will prevent the tiles from pulling too much water from the grout and cause it to dry prematurely.

Use a grout trowel to spread the grout into the joints. (Unlike standard adhesive trowels, the grout trowel has a rubber face so it cannot scratch the tiles. Different versions are available for walls or floors at tile stores and home centers.) Hold the trowel at a 30-degree angle and push the grout into the gaps between the tiles **(6–12)**. It is important to pack the joints to eliminate all voids.

Next, hold the trowel almost perpendicular to the tile surface and work across the tiles to scrape away the excess grout **(6–13)**; but watch that the corners of the tool do not gouge any grout from the joints. While the trowel will pick up and remove most of the excess grout, there will still be a light coating or "haze" on the surface of all the tiles. This must be removed before it begins to harden. The best tool for this is the grout sponge.

Before proceeding to wipe off the remaining grout, wait for 15 to 20 minutes. This waiting period is important because it will allow the grout in the joints to harden so it will not wash out when the sponge passes over. Unfortunately, it is hard to be precise about how long to wait before sponging the surface. If you wait too long, the grout in the cracks will be hard, but the residual grout on the tile surface will be difficult to wipe off. If, on the other hand, you start too soon, the grout in the joints may be damaged. The best course of action is to wait about ten minutes and then test the sponge on a small area.

Some tile setters try to accelerate the grout curing time by dusting the grouted joints with an absorbent power such as grout

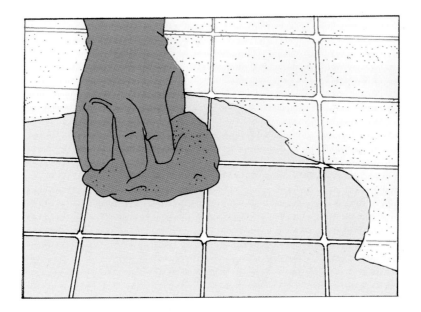

6–14. *The grout trowel will remove most of the excess grout, but some grout will remain in the form of a light haze on the tiles. This must be removed before it dries and hardens. The best tool to use for this is a grout sponge.*

mix, portland cement, or even sawdust. The strategy behind this is that the powder will suck the moisture from the grout and make it dry faster. Indeed it may hasten the drying time, but it will probably cause the grout to cure prematurely and unevenly. This will cause it to crack or deteriorate later on. It is far better to give the grout sufficient time to dry without any accelerators.

The trick to using the sponge to wipe the tile surface is to keep it moist but not dripping. Do this by dipping the sponge into a bucket of clean water and then wringing it out. Also make sure your hands are not dripping. Make a wide sweep across the tiles; then turn the sponge over and make another pass **(6–14)**. Rinse out the sponge, and make sure that all the grit particles lodged in the sponge pores are washed away. Continue wiping the area until all visible grout residue is removed, but remember to keep the sponge clean by rinsing it frequently.

Next, use the round corners of the sponge to dress the grouted joints. Make passes across and down the joints to flatten any peaks or bumps. Ideally the grout joint should be flat and level with the tile surface. This is easy to achieve if the surrounding tiles are relatively flat, but if the edges of the tiles are concave, then the grouted joints will probably be smoothed to a concave cross section.

If you are working on a large area, some of the grout residue may harden before it can be sponged off. In this case, a scouring pad, such as a Scotch-Brite pad, can be used to rub the grout off. Do not use steel wool; it could scratch the surface of the tiles or particles of steel could collect in the grout joint. These particles will eventually rust and discolor the grout.

Sometimes it may be difficult to apply grout with the trowel if the tiles have a textured surface or they have high relief decorations **(6–15)**. Here, the grout would fill into depressions or crannies of the tiles and be almost impossible to remove. The solution, then, is to apply grout with a grout bag.

The grout bag looks like a pastry bag and is used in a similar manner. Grout is loaded into the bag and the top is folded over to contain the contents. The bag is then squeezed to force out a continuous bead of grout—different tips are available to control the width of grout bead.

It's best to work along the full length of a joint, across the entire tiled surface, rather then outlining the perimeter of each tile. This will create a more even fill. After doing all the horizontal joints, do the vertical ones. (This is, of course, for a wall. On a floor where all joints are horizontal, fill the x and then the y axis.) Fill each joint so the grout projects above the tile surface. Use a piece of smooth metal tubing or even your finger (be sure to wear snug-fitting rubber gloves for this) to smooth the joint.

Even after the grout dries completely, it can still be stained by mildew or by colored liquids that are accidentally spilled across the tiles. The best way to keep the grout looking fresh is with regular maintenance and by cleaning up spills promptly. There are a number of products, called sealers, on the market that will seal the grout and make it less susceptible to discoloration.

Sealers fall into two categories: those that coat the surface, and those that penetrate the grout. Both can be water- or solvent-based. Water-based sealers are good

6–15. *Generally, textured tiles with a high relief should not be used in floor installations because they collect dirt and present a walking hazard. (Tiling floors is covered in the next chapter.) In this installation, however, the textured tiles are used in the border and are therefore away from heavy traffic. The color is the same as that of the field tiles, but the symmetrical relief pattern offers a pleasant contrast and serves to emphasize the border.* **(Photo courtesy of Dal–Tile Company)**

for most dry installations, while the solvent-based sealers offer greater protection in wet areas. Depending upon the product, they may change the appearance of the grout and the tiles. Some sealers may darken the material, while others may impart a glossy or semigloss sheen to the tiles and grout. It's important to test all sealers on spare tiles and grout before applying them.

All sealers must be renewed periodically. The penetrating sealers only need to be recoated, but the surface sealers should be removed before a fresh coat is applied. Consult the tile dealer regarding the best type of sealer for your tile installation.

7–1. *Factors to consider when choosing floor tiles are size, shape, color, and texture. The earth tones in these floor tiles create a warm appeal that suggests a Southwestern decorative scheme.*

Tiling Floors

Ceramic tiles are ideal for floor surfaces because they are attractive and durable. They are a good choice in areas that see heavy traffic and in areas where spills and water may be a problem. It is not difficult to install ceramic tile on a floor, provided the floor is reasonably level, square, and flat. In addition, it is essential that the floor be firm and rigid; a floor that bends or flexes too much will cause the tiles to eventually pop up or crack.

CHOOSING FLOOR TILES

Since floor tiles are a relatively permanent surfacing material, it is important to take the time to choose them carefully by considering all the styles and colors available; otherwise you might have to live with a design or pattern that is undesirable. The factors to consider when choosing floor tiles are the size, shape, color, and texture of the tiles.

Floor tiles range in size from 1-inch squares to pieces larger than 24 inches **(7–2)**. Most people find the 6-, 8-, 10-, or 12-inch tiles easiest to work with and maintain. As a general rule, small tiles tend to make a floor look larger **(7–3)**, while the larger tiles can make a large room look smaller **(7–4)**. Smaller tiles will have more grout lines. This often creates a busy pattern on the floor that many people will find distracting. The additional grout around the tiles may also be diffi-

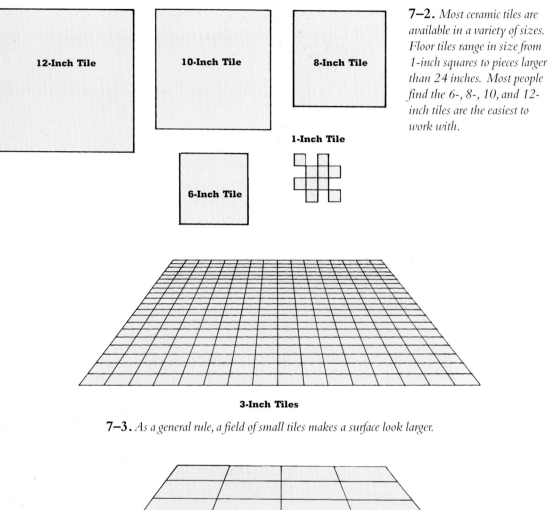

7–2. *Most ceramic tiles are available in a variety of sizes. Floor tiles range in size from 1-inch squares to pieces larger than 24 inches. Most people find the 6-, 8-, 10, and 12-inch tiles are the easiest to work with.*

3-Inch Tiles

7–3. *As a general rule, a field of small tiles makes a surface look larger.*

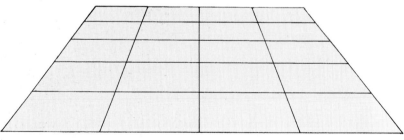

12-Inch Tiles

7–4. *A field of large tiles makes a surface look smaller.*

cult to keep clean in busy rooms like the kitchen, where spills are a definite possibility. One size of tile doesn't have to be used when planning a floor pattern. It is possible to mix sizes in any installation. Large tiles can be used in the main field and the borders filled with small tiles, or a central pattern of small tiles can be made that is surrounded with larger pieces.

Of course, tiles are available in the standard square shape. This is the easiest shape to work with, and it offers the widest choice of

7–5. *Patterns and colors in tile installations do not have to be bold to be effective. Here the field is composed of tiles in three shapes: squares, large and small, and rectangles. A few small squares in a contrasting tone are added to provide additional visual interest. The overall effect is a design that is pleasing but not so obvious that it distracts the eye from the focal point of the room.* **(Photo courtesy of M.E. Tile Company)**

sizes, colors, and textures. Square tiles give a surface an organized and formal look, and if an individual tile has to be replaced later on, it will be easy to find the same shape and size (it may be difficult to match the exact color, but you can sometimes get around this by using a few contrasting tiles to create a pattern in the field). Still, as long as you are in the planning stage, it is worth looking into the wide variety of shapes that manufacturers offer, if only to explore the fascinating design possibilities for the home **(7–5)**.

In contrast to the precise look of square tiles, tiles with irregular shapes offer a casual and rustic charm that works well in less formal rooms. Also bear in mind that because most tiles are square, any floor with unusually shaped tiles will immediately attract attention.

Besides a rectangular shape **(7–6)**, tiles are available in diamonds, triangles, ogees (some-

times called Provençal tiles), as triple tomettes (a grouping of three diamonds), elongated hexagons often called lozenges, and eight-point stars (sometimes called Byzantine tiles). In addition, some tile manufacturers offer standard tiles with scored backs. The tile setter can change the shape of the tile by breaking it along the scored line.

Many of the different shapes are interlocking, so it is possible to form complex patterns by joining different tiles. Novice tile setters will find this challenging at best, and they should spend time developing a working plan on paper before attempting any complex installation.

In most cases the term "shape" refers to the outline of the tiles, but it can also refer to the profile or cross section of the piece. We

7–6. *At first glance, this installation looks like a standard floor pattern, but there is a variation that adds to visual interest to the floor. Rectangular tiles with a low relief are added to the field or square tiles. The result is a subtle interplay of shape and texture that makes the floor interesting but not distracting.*

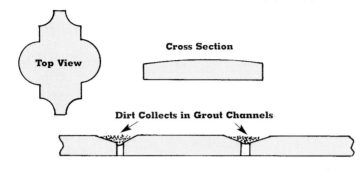

7–7. *The term "shape" usually refers to the outline of the tiles, but it can also refer to the profile or cross section of the piece. We tend to think of tiles as having a flat surface from one side to the other, but some tiles are beveled around the edges. Called "pillow" tiles, they form an irregular surface when set together. The downside to this surface is that the edges adjacent to the grout joints are recessed. These joints often collect dirt and are difficult to keep clean.*

7–8. *An interesting pattern and contrasting colors serve to make this floor installation especially attractive. The border tiles are large squares laid in a jack-on-jack arrangement. The central field tiles are laid in a herringbone pattern. While this is a handsome pattern, it necessitates more tile cutting and requires more tiles than a traditional arrangement.*

tend to think of tiles as having a flat surface from one end to the other, but some tiles are beveled around the edges. Called "pillow" tiles, they form an irregular surface when set together **(7–7)**. The effect is a subtle visual interplay between light and shadow that can vary as the lighting changes. The downside to pillow tiles is that their beveled edges create recessed grout joints. These deep joints often collect dirt and may be difficult to keep clean,

so tiles with beveled edges are not a good choice in areas that receive heavy traffic.

Choosing the right color may be the most difficult choice of all, because the color can dramatically change the atmosphere of an entire room **(7–8)**. There are no hard and fast rules when it comes to picking a good color, but there are some general guidelines that will prove helpful. Dark colors tend to make a room look smaller, while light ones open a room up. Light colors **(7–9)** will show dirt more than middle tones, while dark shades of blue, green, and maroon will show dust and footprints.

7–9. *Light-colored tiles can make a room look brighter and larger. However, they show dirt more than dark-colored tiles. This is not a problem with the floor tiles in this room, because they have a variegated color that will not show dirt as readily as monochromatic floor tiles.*

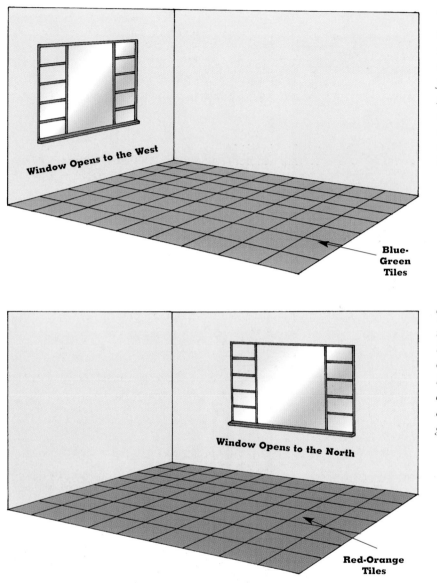

7–10. *Rooms that receive direct sunlight, that is, those with eastern or western exposures, benefit from tiles with blue or green colors. These will create the effect of a cool atmosphere to counteract the heat of the harsh sunlight.*

Window Opens to the West

Blue-Green Tiles

7–11. *Rooms with a northern exposure can look warmer with red or orange tiles. Warm colors like red, pink, and peach complement skin tones and give people a healthy glow.*

Window Opens to the North

Red-Orange Tiles

In general, floor tiles that are a darker hue than the surrounding walls add focus by creating a "ground" for the entire color scheme. Normally this is ideal, but it can backfire if the room has a number of dark accents. Consider, for example, a kitchen with cabinets of dark wood; adding a dark tile floor could make the room feel small and oppressive. Here, it may be better to go in the opposite direction and install a floor with light-colored tiles.

Rooms that receive direct sunlight can often benefit from the cooler color hues of blue and green **(7–10)**, while rooms with a northern exposure can be warmed with reds and pinks **(7–11)**. Warm colors like red, pink, and peach complement skin tones and give people a healthy glow, so they are ideal colors

7–12. *Large green tiles are used for this floor. The color is repeated in the counter tiles, but the counter installation uses smaller tiles. The smaller tiles fit the counter better and, at the same time, prevent it from looking too "monolithic."* **(Photo courtesy of Lis King Tile Company)**

ate an atmosphere of subtle warmth yet do not show dirt or stains readily.

But color does not exist in a vacuum, and it is impossible to choose colored tiles simply by looking in a sample book or around a showroom. These tiles may look fine in isolated areas, but they can take on a different tone and complexion when placed in a room. Every color is affected by the surrounding colors. Opposite colors like blue and orange will intensify each other's effect, while neighboring colors like green and blue will create a sense of harmony and serenity. It's essential when choosing any tile color to purchase a few samples to get some idea of how they will look in relation to the surrounding room **(7–12)**.

In contrast to color, texture is a subtle design element, but it can still have an enor-

for the bathroom. Psychological tests show that red stimulates the appetite, so it can be an effective color for the dining room, although this may not be a good choice for people on a diet.

Yellow is an active color and can be used to effectively brighten a kitchen or utility room. It is also a good choice for a hallway or foyer because it has a cheery, welcoming quality. Psychologists report that exposure to yellow surfaces for extended periods has a tendency to make people restless or uncomfortable, so it is not a good choice for dining rooms, living rooms, or any room designed for relaxation.

Pure white can often look sterile and antiseptic, and it may be difficult to keep some white floor tiles clean. Fortunately, there are many shades of off-white that cre-

7–13. *Generally glazed tiles are not a good choice for floor installations because they do not offer enough traction and present a slipping hazard. However, they can be safely used in low-traffic areas.*

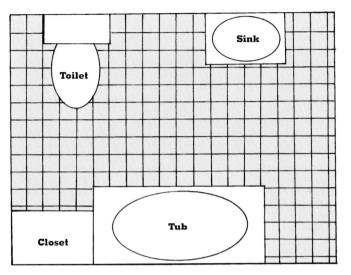

7–14. *Estimating the amount of tiles need-ed to cover a floor surface can be problematic in rooms with irregular walls or in rooms like bathrooms that have permanent fixtures mounted on the floor. It is easier to figure the quantity of tiles needed with a detailed floor plan drawn to scale. Any paper can be used for the plan, but it easier and more accurate to use graph paper.*

mous impact on the room. Glazed tiles make a room look brighter and larger **(7–13)**. Tiles with a matte finish will make a room look more cozy and intimate. Some tiles, such as Mexican pavers, have a rough, uneven surface texture, and they can make a room look rustic and casual.

Part of choosing the right tile for the floor also includes selecting a grout that comple-ments it. Grout choice involves deciding on a good color and also deciding on the ideal width for the gap between the tiles. These may seem like subtle or insignificant details, but different grout patterns can dramatically change the entire effect of the floor tiles in a room. If, for example, the grout is in stark contrast to the tiles, say, dark tiles surrounded by light grout, the grid pattern is emphasized; and the floor surface will become a dominant element in the entire room.

PLANNING THE LAYOUT

Before purchasing the tiles, you should have some idea of how many are needed. Most tile manufacturers offer a rough guide for their products. It is basically a recommendation for how many tiles will be needed to cover a square foot of surface area. This can certainly be useful for simple floor plans, but the guide is based on a grout-width measurement arbi-trarily assigned by the manufacturers. Your design may have wider or narrower grout widths, and this could throw off the final esti-mate. In addition, a simple square foot esti-mate does not take into account the number of border tiles that may have to be cut or any fixtures that may have to be worked around.

A more accurate method of estimating the final tile count would be to make a detailed, scaled drawing of the final layout and use it to count the actual number of tiles needed **(7–14)**. The scaled drawing will also help you to visualize the final installation so any potential problems can be anticipated and solved beforehand. Of course, the draw-ing can be made on any type of paper, but it is easier and more accurate to use graph paper. It will help you to get right angles, calculate the area of the room, and pinpoint any irreg-ularities between the walls, floor, and fixtures.

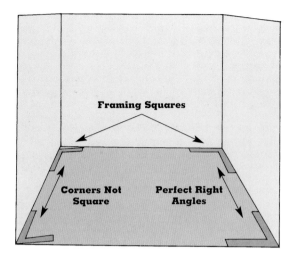

7–15. *Before installing the floor tiles, check carefully to make sure the room is square. Use a carpenter's square to ensure that each corner forms a 90-degree angle.*

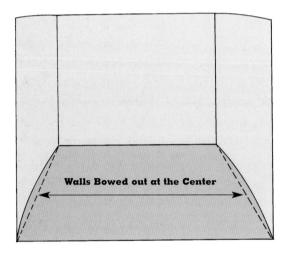

7–16. *Even if the room is exactly or almost square, the walls may not be straight. They may be bowed or curved. These deviations can affect the final installation. Use a straightedge or taut string to check the walls.*

Start by taking accurate measurements of the room. The measurements should include the length and width of the room, the width and location of all doors, and installed fixtures or cabinets.

Next, check to see whether the floor is square **(7–15)**. If the room is small, a framing square can be used in each corner to determine that the corners are at right angles. For larger rooms, it may be more convenient and accurate to adopt the Pythagorean theorem as a measuring device; mark off three equal increments (these may be 12, 18, or even 24 inches wide) on one wall, and four of the same increment on the adjacent wall. Connect the two points with a string or straightedge. If the corner is a true right angle, the string will be exactly five increments wide.

Even if the room is exactly or almost square, the walls may not be straight; they may be bowed or curved. These deviations can effect the final installation, especially if you try to line a row of tiles up against that wall. A preliminary check for straightness can be made by sighting the entire wall surface, near the floor level. It is important to sketch the deviations of any distorted wall on the scale drawing. A simple way to capture the profile of the wall is by snapping a chalk line parallel to the wall and then taking measurements from the line to the wall at various points **(7–16)**. Transfer these measurements to the scale drawing.

Finally, check to make sure the floor is level. An out-of-level floor will not affect the final tile installation, unless you plan to run tiles up the walls, but it could indicate that the underlying support is weak and may need additional bracing. Be sure to investigate this possibility before proceeding too far into the installation.

Another advantage of graph paper is that it can be used to determine how many tile "units" are needed for the floor. A tile unit is the width and length of one full tile plus the

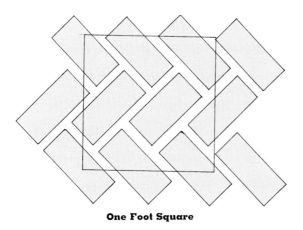

One Foot Square

7–17. *It is difficult to estimate the quantity of tiles for a floor installation if they will be arranged in a complex pattern. Begin by calculating the area of the floor in square feet. Then lay out tiles in the planned arrangement, leaving space for the grout. Next, measure how many tiles will fit in a one-foot square. Multiply that number by the total area.*

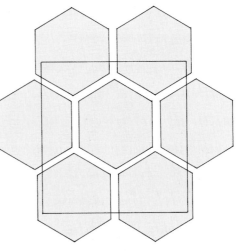

One Foot Square

7–18. *It is also difficult to estimate the quantity of tiles for a floor installation if they have an irregular shape. Use the same calculating method described in the previous caption.*

respective grout joints. If square tiles are being used, then it's a simple matter to assign a square on the grid paper for each tile. If rectangular tiles of different lengths and widths will be used, then it becomes a matter of using the appropriate number of boxes to match the width/length ratio of the tile. If, for example, the tiles are 3 inches wide and 6 inches long, then two adjacent grid squares will represent one tile.

The situation becomes a little more difficult if irregularly shaped tiles are being used. However, it can be simplified by laying some of the actual tiles out on a piece of paper that has a 1-foot square box drawn on it. Lay the tiles out in the planned arrangement, leaving space for the grout joint **(7–17** and **7–18)**. Now you can see how many tiles will be needed to fill a square foot, and the grid paper can be used to determine the number of square feet in the room.

Another way to estimate the number of tiles needed is by measuring the room with a layout stick. Since the layout stick is divided into tile units, you can see how many units will fit across the width of the room and along its length. Multiply these two numbers together to get the total quantity of tiles needed for the installation.

This number represents the number of tiles that it will take to cover the floor surface, but it doesn't take into account the number of tiles needed to replace those that break or are improperly cut. The rule of thumb is to take the total tile estimate and then add 10 percent to that figure. The extra tiles become a reserve stock. They might be needed if the correct quantity is underestimated, or they can be used to replace any miscalculations, breakage, or miscuts that occur during installation.

The reserve stock figure is just a rough

guideline. It can be changed depending upon the confidence you have in your calculations and in your abilities to put down tile without mistakes. If you are reasonably confident that all will go exactly as planned, you can reduce the order to 5 percent more than calculated. If you're less optimistic, then increase the amount.

Before placing the order, it's a good idea to check with the tile dealer and see whether he has a return policy, that is, if he will refund your money for returns of unopened cartons. Also, find out how easy it is to get more tiles if they are needed. If the tiles are readily available, then it's possible to get by with fewer spares, ordering more only when they are needed. If, on the other hand, the tiles are produced in a limited run, it's advisable to have a larger quantity on hand in case replacements are needed in the future.

Estimating the amount of adhesive needed is not as complicated as estimating the tile count. You simply need to know the number of square feet of floor surface to be covered; then check the labels on the adhesive container. It will have coverage figures that will guide you. Estimating the amount of grout is slightly more difficult because it depends on the width of the grout joint. Here, it's best to discuss your plans with the tile dealer. He can check your figures and make suggestions on the amount to buy. When purchasing adhesive and grout, it is better to buy extra than to run out in the middle of the job.

The next step is to return to the scale drawing and work out the actual placement for the tile field. To some people this may seem almost academic, but taking the time to work out the floor plan can often mean the difference between a perfect job and one that is an eyesore. With an installation of patterned or colorful tiles, the visual impact of the room can be swayed by the placement of the tiles.

There are no hard and fast rules for proper placement, but there are a few common-sense guidelines that are worth considering. First look at the room carefully to determine whether there is a visual focal point; it may be a fireplace, a picture window, or simply a strong architectural feature. Not all rooms have focal points, but if your room does, then center the tile field around it. Position all cut and narrow tiles (border tiles are an exception) away from this point. Use only full tiles around doorways and entrances.

In most layouts, tiles will have to be cut at the borders. No tile should be cut to less than

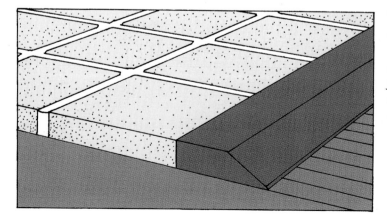

7–19. *A tile bed will raise the surface of a floor. This may be a problem with thick tiles, at door openings, or where the tile floor connects with an untiled floor. An easy way to resolve the difference in height between the two floors is to install a beveled threshold.*

half its size. This problem can usually be avoided by shifting the field slightly. This shift will result in a more symmetrical field having cut tiles of equal widths on opposite walls.

Another thing to consider in your plans is the possible rise in the floor level and its effect on adjacent floors. The new tiles will make the floor a little higher, and this change will be noticeable at doorways and other places where the tile floor connects with an untiled floor. An easy way to resolve these differences in height is to install a threshold or border between the two surfaces **(7–19)**. The threshold may be made of wood, metal, or marble and can be beveled or slanted from one level to the other. Since the threshold will probably have to be custom-made, it's best to hold off installing it until the tile job is complete.

PREPARING THE ROOM

Theoretically, when the floor surface is properly prepared, the installation of the tiles can begin, but sometimes it is helpful to also remove the doors, radiators, and other items that obstruct the working area. At first, this may seem like a lot of unnecessary work, but the entire tile installation will be easier and neater if the time is taken to prepare the room first.

Start by removing the door to the room. Usually this is a matter of pulling out the hinge pins. There are two reasons to take the door down: First, it will make it easier to tile around the entranceway without having to reposition the door as you work; and second, the tiles will undoubtedly raise the level of the floor, so the bottom of the door may have to be trimmed. This should be done with the door lying flat (but wait until the tile floor is down, so you can be sure of

the amount that will have to be trimmed).

Close the entranceway to the room by erecting a curtain of plastic sheeting. Use duct tape at the top and along one side of the plastic. This curtain will prevent any dust from spreading to other parts of the house.

Next, empty the room of all furniture. Even though only the floor is being worked on, it is likely that mixing adhesives and grout could raise some dust, so cover all switch plates and outlets with plastic wrap. Seal the edges of the wrap with either masking or duct tape. Then remove or cover any drapery around the windows.

Next, remove the molding around the baseboard. If the molding is relatively new, it can be pried away from the wall with a pry bar. Before pushing the pry bar into the molding, position a wide putty knife against the wall **(7–20)**. This will shield the wall to keep the pry bar from denting or damaging it.

It's best to work with a few wedges in

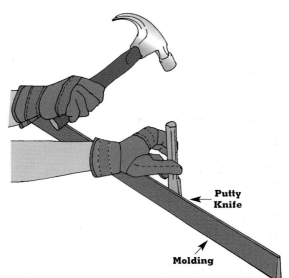

→ **Putty Knife**

↗ **Molding**

7–20. *Use a chisel or stiff putty knife to open a gap between the molding and the wall. Work carefully to avoid damaging either the wall or the molding.*

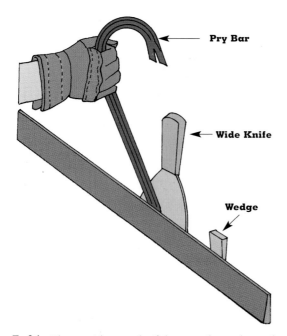

7–21. *Place a wide putty knife between the pry bar and the wall surface. This will protect the wall surface and prevent the pry bar from denting or damaging it. While pulling the molding away from the wall, insert a wooden wedge to hold the gap open. Move the bar to another position and work the molding away from the wall. This "pry-and-wedge" technique will allow you to remove an entire strip of molding without breaking it.*

addition to the bar. As you start to pull the molding free with the bar, insert a wedge; then move the bar farther along and pry at another place. Add more wedges while working the molding from the wall. This "pry-and-wedge" technique will allow an entire strip of molding to be removed without breaking it **(7–21)**.

Of course, if the existing molding is scuffed or shabby looking you may elect to replace it; in this case, there is no need to be careful when pulling it away from the walls. On the other hand, if the molding is older and difficult to replace, a different strategy may have to be adopted for removal.

Attempting to pry up old molding can damage it. A good way to free the molding is by driving the holding nails through the molding into the wall. This will free the molding so it can be pulled away. Use a narrow nail set and hammer for this.

If the floor originally had resilient flooring, there may be a vinyl topset base (this is essentially a strip of vinyl that functions as molding) around the bottom of the walls. The vinyl topset base is held in place with adhesive, not nails. To remove it, first soften the adhesive by heating the base with a heat gun. Adjust the heat gun for a low temperature setting and move it along the vinyl base without focusing too long on one place. Use a wide putty knife to pry the base from the wall.

After the molding is off, remove all floor cabinets and floor-mounted plumbing fixtures (the toilet, for example, or radiators, unless you are going to tile around them). Before disconnecting any plumbing, make sure that all appropriate water-supply lines are closed. Unless the shutoff valves are in the room, they should be labeled so that no one turns on the water when you are working.

After the tile installation is complete, the molding, door, and fixtures can be replaced. The molding and door may have to be trimmed or repositioned to accommodate the new floor height.

Removing and Replacing the Toilet in the Bathroom

It is not always necessary to remove the toilet. Instead, the tiles can be run to the perimeter of the toilet base. This will be perfectly adequate as long as the existing toilet remains in place. If the toilet has to be changed in the future, you may find that the base of the new fixture does not fit within the depression left in the tile floor. Then more tiles will have to be added to that area if a new toilet with the same base profile as the old one cannot be found.

In the final analysis, it may be best to remove the toilet and then replace it after the floor is installed. In some residences—particularly co-ops and condominiums—the flush mechanism for the toilet is a flush valve. In this case, neither the bowl nor the flush valve has to be removed unless the floor will be tiled. In this event, consult the chapter on tiling a bathroom floor. Tile installation will consist of cutting the tiles to fit around the inlet pipe for the valve.

The standard two-piece tank-bowl configuration (a two-piece model is called a *closed-coupled toilet*) has the tank attached to the bowl with two bolts. Before attempting to remove the tank, shut off the water at the supply valve; then empty the tank by holding the trip handle. This will flush out most of the water, but some water will remain in the tank. Remove this by sopping it up with a sponge.

The tank is held in place with two bolts that go through the tank bottom and through the bowl flange. Remove the two nuts inside the base of the tank to loosen the bolts. If they are badly corroded, you may have to saw the bolts off with a hacksaw blade or break the nuts with a nut cracker (available at auto supply stores). After removing the bolts, move to the supply line and disconnect it from the tank. Now the tank can be lifted off the bowl.

A wall-mounted tank rests on a flange attached to the wall **(7–22)**. The only connection to the bowl is an L-shaped pipe. As

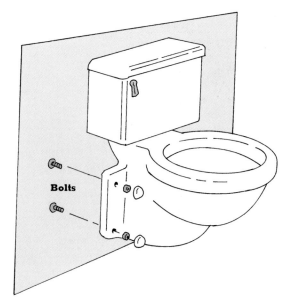

7–22. *A wall-mounted toilet is attached to the wall with four bolts—two on each side of the bowl. To remove the toilet, shut off and disconnect the supply line, unscrew the nuts, and pull the toilet away from the wall. Removing a wall-mounted toilet may not be necessary if there is enough clearance beneath the toilet to install the floor tiles. In cramped quarters, it is probably a good idea to remove the toilet so there is adequate room to work.*

with the closed-coupled model, the first step is to shut off the water supply and then empty the tank. Next, loosen the flange nuts on the supply pipe at the tank inlet and at the bowl inlet. Now the pipe can be removed. Next, remove the supply tube from the tank. Finally, lift the tank from the wall flange.

Removing the tank may provide enough clearance to tile the wall, so the bowl may not have to be removed. If more room is needed, however, remove the bowl.

Removing the bowl is relatively easy once the tank is off. The bowl is held in place with two hold-down bolts on each side of the bowl (also called closet bolts). Often these are concealed beneath two porcelain caps. Pry off the caps and loosen the nuts on the bolt.

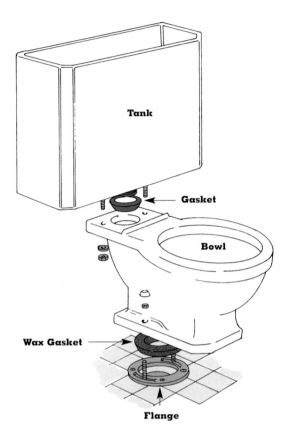

7–23. *Replacing a toilet is essentially the same process as removing it, only in reverse. Look at the two bolts projecting upward from the floor flange. If they are in good condition, leave them in place. If they are corroded, they should be replaced. If you use replacement parts, check to make sure they are rust-resistant. When replacing the toilet, be sure to use a new wax gasket.*

On older toilets, these nuts may be corroded and difficult to remove. In this case, saw through the bolts with a hacksaw blade. Be careful when sawing not to scratch the finish on the base of the bowl. It may be possible to pull the bowl up from the floor at this point. If it proves stubborn, however, the seal around the base may be holding it in place. Run a stiff putty knife between the base and the floor to break the seal.

When the bowl is pulled off, the drainpipe

will be exposed. It is a good idea to loosely stuff a rag in the drain orifice to close it; otherwise, debris could fall into the pipe and clog it.

These above procedures describe the removal of a two-piece bowl-tank unit. Some toilets have the toilet bowl and tank molded as one unit. Removal procedures are basically the same. First, shut off the supply valve and empty water from the tank. Then remove the supply tube. At this point, disconnect the hold-down nuts on the bowl and lift the one-piece tank-bowl unit off. A word of caution, however: these toilets are heavier than the two-piece models; enlist the aid of a helper before attempting to move a unit of this type.

There is another type of toilet; this is a wall-mounted toilet. With this toilet, there is no need to remove the tank because the bowl and tank are connected together and mounted to firm supports in the wall. The simplest models are held in place with only two bolts. It is only necessary to loosen the bolts and pull the toilet free. A wall-mounted toilet is heavy and will require two people to lift it from the wall.

If you cannot figure how a toilet is secured in place, consult with a plumber or leave it in place and cut the tiles to fit around it.

Replacing the toilet is essentially the same process as removing it, only in reverse **(7–23)**. There is one small change that will have to be made before the toilet can be reinstalled. The mounting flange on the floor will be lower after the tiles are installed. This will create a gap between the base of the new toilet and the flange surface. Before the new toilet can be installed, the flange must be brought to the level of the surrounding tiles **(7–24)**. This means removing the old flange and replacing it with a thicker one. This is a wise move if the old flange appears corroded or damaged in any way. In addition to the flange, you must buy a wax gasket. The gasket forms the seal around the toilet horn to prevent leaks.

Look also at the two bolts projecting upward from the flange. These are called the closet bolts. They can be used provided they are in good condition. If the bolts are rusted or corroded, they should be replaced. (New closet bolts are needed even if you are buying a new toilet, as they are not part of the hardware kit that comes with the new toilet.) Whether you are buying a new toilet or replacing the old one, it is a wise precaution to check all the hardware to see that it is rust-resistant. An easy way to do this is by holding a magnet to the piece. If it is attracted to the magnet, it is probably ferric metal and can corrode. If the hardware is not rust-resistant, it should be replaced.

If the flange looks okay and there were no leakage problems with the old bowl, you can keep the flange in place and install a special wax gasket with a plastic extension ring on the toilet horn.

Plumbers differ on whether it is better to place the gasket onto the horn and then push the toilet in place on the floor flange, or position the gasket on the flange and lower the toilet onto it. Either method will work provided the toilet is maneuvered carefully onto the flange to avoid damaging or distorting the soft wax gasket. Turn the bowl upright and lower it slowly onto the closet bolts.

Some books suggest that you press down

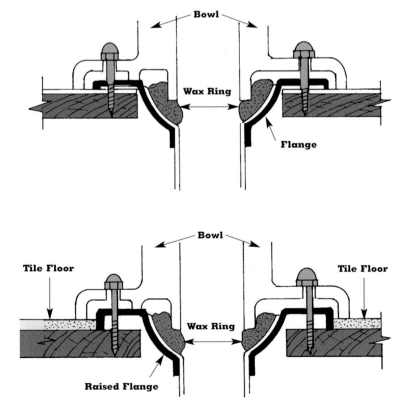

7–24. *There is one small change that will have to be made before the toilet can be reinstalled. The mounting flange on the floor will be lower after the tiles are installed. This will create a gap between the base of the new toilet and the flange surface. Before the new toilet can be installed, the flange must be brought to the level of the surrounding tiles. This can be done by removing the old flange and replacing it with a thicker one.*

hard with your full weight to seat the bowl and shape the gasket to make a watertight seal. Should you try this, be very careful to apply even pressure to the toilet rim. If you lean too hard on one side, the wax gasket will distort and it will not form a watertight seal. Also, be careful of applying too much pressure; this could also distort the wax gasket.

A better way to seat the bowl is by tightening the nuts on the closet bolts. Start on one side and give the nut five or six turns; then move to other side and do the same. Repeat this alternate tightening routine until the bowl is snug to the floor. Do not tighten these nuts too much or the bowl could crack.

The next step is to mount the tank onto the bowl. The installation procedure for the tank is straightforward (detailed instructions should be included with the toilet hardware). Invert the tank so the large opening, the flush-valve outlet, mates with the inlet opening on the rear of the toilet rim. Push the two tank bolts through the tank bottom and bowl rim. Align the tank so it is parallel with the rear wall and then tighten the bolts. Hook up the supply tube to the inlet opening under the tank and turn on the water.

The last step is to draw a bead of caulk around the base of the toilet and the finished floor. It is a good idea, however, to wait a week before doing this. This will allow time to inspect the toilet base for any leaks that may occur around the wax seal. With the caulk bead in place, these leaks may be blocked and run under the floor, where they will remain undetected until the water damages the ceiling below.

PREPARING THE SUBFLOOR

Probably the hardest part of installing the tile floor will be preparing the subfloor, but before working on the floor consider the rest of the room. If the entire room will be finished, hold off the floor work until the ceiling and walls are done. Work on the floor last, so it does not get damaged or stained.

If you are moving into a new home and have alerted the builder to your plans, then the proper subfloor will be finished and waiting. However, check it to make sure it is square, level, flat, and strong enough to support the tiles. Older floors, whether they are wood strips or concrete, will require more work.

Some tile setters will install ceramic tiles over a wood strip floor, but this can present problems because wood expands and contracts at different rates than the tile. It is advisable then to remove the flooring and place backer board over the subfloor.

Before installing the backer board, inspect the subfloor. Make sure it is firmly attached to the floor joists. If not, nail it in place with spiral flooring nails. In some spots, the subfloor may be slightly raised so there is a gap between it and the joist underneath. Here, it's best to insert shims or thin wedges in the gap to keep the floor from flexing. Do not, however, drive the wedges in too hard; you may raise that part of the floor too high and create a noticeable bump. The wedges must be installed from below where the joists are exposed.

If the floor feels "springy," it may be the joist below has moved down and away, creating a gap between it and several boards. The best way to close the gap is by nailing a piece of 1 X 4 alongside the joist so it supports the floorboards above. This extra board, called a "sister" board, can be nailed in place with 8d nails.

While you are working underneath, inspect the bridging between the joists. Bridging is the narrow boards nailed diagonally between the joists. They prevent the joists from shifting laterally. If any bridge pieces seem weak, either renail or replace them.

Of course, all this maintenance is possible only if the joists can be approached from beneath, that is, if the floor to be tiled is directly above an unfinished basement. If not, the floor can only be worked on from above. Here, you are restricted to driving nails or screws through the floor into the joists below.

Concrete provides an excellent base for ceramic tile, but it can also present problems. Moisture is a problem because it can penetrate into the tile adhesive and affect the bond. Surface moisture from condensed humidity or from a spill is not a problem. All that needs to be done is wait until the floor has time to dry out.

A more serious problem is moisture that comes from groundwater penetrating through the concrete. Even if the concrete floor is allowed to dry out, the problem will reoccur whenever rainwater builds up in the earth surrounding the house. If you are unsure whether moisture is coming from the ambient humidity or from groundwater, make the following test.

Tape a sheet of plastic wrap, about 2 feet square, to the floor, and seal the edges with duct tape. If, after 24 hours, drops of condensation appear under the plastic, then groundwater is the culprit and the floor is probably too damp for tile installation.

Still, the problem may not be hopeless.

Consult a professional contractor to see whether the problem can be solved by installing a good drainage system. In some cases, if the moisture problem is not too serious, it may be cured with an application of concrete sealer.

When the concrete floor is dry, inspect it for cracks, holes, and bumps. Hairline cracks do not have to be filled. Wide cracks must be filled. First they should be enlarged with a cold chisel. (Remember whenever chiseling concrete to first don goggles and heavy gloves. Also wear a dust mask when grinding concrete.) Undercut into the crack. This will provide a key for the patching cement. When it hardens, it will be firmly locked under the edges of the crack.

Use water and a stiff brush to wash out the crack and remove all loose debris. Dampen the edges of the crack with either water or a latex bonding liquid and then fill the cavity with patching cement. Use a small trowel to push the patching cement into the crack and to force it into the undercut cavities. Finally, smooth the patch over and feather the edges so they blend with the surrounding area. Before the patch hardens, check the work with a straightedge to be sure that it is even with the rest of the floor.

Any bumps on the concrete surface should be leveled to make them even with the surrounding floor. Small bumps or irregularities may be removed with a cold chisel. High spots in the surface can be ground down with a belt or disc sander until the spot is level with the surrounding area.

To ensure a good bond with the thinset adhesive, the concrete surface should have some "tooth" so the adhesive can create a

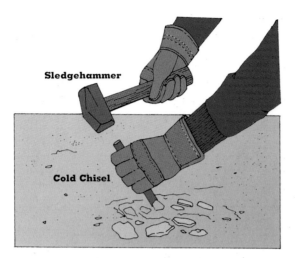

7–25. *To patch a large hole or damaged area in a concrete floor, you will first have to prepare it to receive the fresh concrete. Use a chisel and small sledgehammer to break up any large pieces of concrete so they can be lifted out and discarded. Next, undercut the edges of the hole with a chisel; then excavate the hole until the bottom is at least four inches deeper than the base of the concrete floor. It may not be necessary to excavate to this depth if the damage is relatively shallow or if the floor is especially thick.*

mechanical bond. "Tooth" is simply a rough or textured surface. Most concrete floors are fine as is, but some have smooth or even painted surfaces. These should be sanded with coarse grit paper to roughen the surface. It is possible to do this with a belt sander if the floor is relatively small, but for larger floors it is best to rent a floor sander.

After sanding, vacuum the floor and then wash it with commercial concrete or driveway cleaner (not a blacktop cleaner). Finally, rinse it thoroughly with clean water. When the floor is completely dry, it is ready for the tile installation.

In rare cases, there may be a concrete floor with a major problem such as a deep depression or a large hole. It is possible to fill the depression with concrete, but you cannot always be sure that the new concrete will achieve a firm bond with the floor. In this case, it may actually be better to break into the floor and create a hole to fill.

In order to patch a large hole in a concrete floor, you will have to prepare it to receive the fresh concrete **(7–25)**. First, remove any broken concrete in the hole. Use a sledgehammer to break up any large pieces of concrete so they can be lifted out and discarded. Next, undercut the edges of the hole with a chisel; then excavate the hole until the bottom is at least four inches deeper than the base of the concrete floor. Fill the hole with

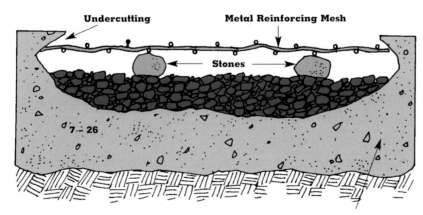

7–26. *Fill the hole with enough gravel to come up to the bottom of the concrete floor. Cut a piece of reinforcing wire mesh the size of the cavity—ideally the ends of the mesh wires should butt against the walls of the hole. The mesh should rest a few inches above the gravel so it will be centered in the patch. An easy way to do this is by placing a few pieces of concrete or brick under the mesh so it rests off the gravel.*

gravel until it is flush with the bottom of the concrete floor **(7–26)**.

Cut a piece of reinforcing wire mesh the size of the cavity; the ends of the mesh wires should butt the walls of the hole. Ideally, the mesh should rest a few inches above the gravel so it will be centered in the concrete patch. An easy way to accomplish this is by placing a few pieces of concrete or brick under the mesh so it rests above the gravel.

Mix the concrete, but before pouring it, dampen the walls of the hole with water or a latex bonding agent. Pour the concrete into the hole, making sure to force it into the cavities under the edges of the hole. Add a little extra concrete to the pour to allow for depressions as it settles **(7–27)**.

The next step is to level the patch **(7–28)**. Use a 2 × 4 that is longer than the width of the hole as a leveling tool (commonly called a "screed"). Move the 2 × 4 laterally back and forth while pushing it across the surface of the patch. This action will slice off the high mounds of concrete and push them into the depressions. Normally, when pouring a concrete patch or slab, the final step would be to smooth the surface with a "float," but this step is unnecessary because here it is better to leave the surface of the patch slightly rough so the tile adhesive will bond with it.

Newly poured concrete needs time to cure. Curing is accomplished by keeping the new concrete damp and allowing it to slowly dry and harden. Dampen the surface of the patch and cover it with polyethylene to prevent the moisture from evaporating. Keep the patch covered and allow it to cure for at least a week.

You may want to put tile over a floor that is already tiled. Is this possible? Yes, provided

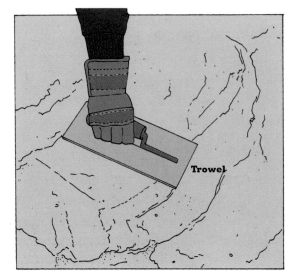

7–27. *Mix the concrete patch before pouring it; then dampen the walls of the hole with water or a latex bonding agent. Pour the concrete into the hole, making sure to force it in the cavities under the edges of the hole. Add a little extra concrete to the pour to allow for depression as the concrete settles. Use a trowel to smooth the patch.*

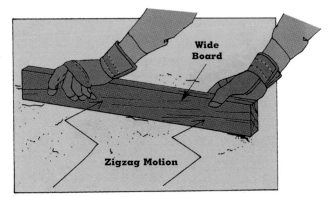

7–28. *The next step is to level the patch. Use a wide board as a leveling tool, commonly called a "screed." Move the board laterally back and forth while pushing it across the patch. This action will slice off the high mounds of concrete and push them into any depressions.*

that the tiles in place are in good condition. So the first step is to carefully examine the tile floor and look for cracked or loose tiles. If the tiles or the grout lines are cracked, that is, if a number of tiles in one area are cracked, it usually indicates a weak subfloor or a damaged underlayment. Remove the damaged tiles and make all necessary corrections to the substrate below before proceeding with the installation.

If a few loose tiles are present, pick them up and butter the backs with the same adhesive that will be used for the new tile installation. Press the tiles back into place, making sure that they are no higher than the surrounding tiles. If there are a large number of loose tiles, it may be better to pull all the remaining tiles up and install the new tiles directly on the substrate.

Next, look at the grout joints. If they are recessed below the surface of the tiles, they should be filled to bring them level. This is done by adding more grout, but first the existing grout joints should be coated with an adhesive. The local tile dealer can recommend a good product for this task. Leveling the grout joints is not necessary if a mortar-based thinset adhesive will be used for the new tiles, because the mortar-based thinset will fill in the grout joint depressions when it is put down.

In order to ensure a good bond between the adhesive and the existing tiles, it will be necessary to roughen the surface and create a "tooth" for the adhesive to grip. Use a belt sander with silicon-carbide paper for this. Be sure to wear goggles and a dust mask for this operation. In the corners and other hard-to-reach areas, use a sanding block or a Carborundum stone to roughen the tiles. After sanding, vacuum up all the dust.

It may be necessary to prime the tiles before applying the adhesive (look on the package for the manufacturer's recommendations). Use a foam-rubber roller to apply the primer.

POURING A CONCRETE FLOOR

If an existing wood floor is thick enough, it should theoretically be stable enough to support a tile installation. Still, many tile installers point out that wood has one disadvantage when it comes to supporting tiles. Since wood is greatly affected by the temperature and humidity cycle, it expands and contracts at a different rate than the tile on top. Tile has less porosity then wood, so it expands very little. This expansion/contraction cycle, they feel, will eventually be transmitted through to the tiles and result in popped tiles or cracks in the grout joints.

One way to avoid this problem is by installing backer board. It provides a more stable base than the wood, but its main disadvantage is that there will be joints between the panels and these could affect the tile installed on top.

Many tile installers feel that the best tile substrate is a layer of poured concrete, commonly called "mud" among tile installers. This, they say, has a minor expansion/contraction cycle and offers greater stability for a tile floor. The main disadvantage to a mud floor is that it will raise the level of the floor so it is no longer level with the other floors that connect to it. Even though this is a problem, it can often be minimized by installing tapered thresholds at the connection points.

Before the concrete can be poured, it is necessary to install a waterproof membrane to protect and insulate the wood subfloor **(7–29)**. Fifteen-pound building felt (often called tar paper) can be used for this. Overlap the seams of the felt paper by at least 5 inches. Attach the felt to the underlayment by driving staples every 6 to 8 inches apart.

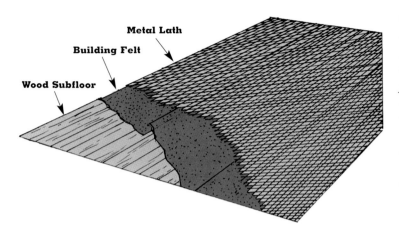

Metal Lath

Building Felt

Wood Subfloor

7–29. Pouring concrete over a wooden floor can be problematic if the floor is not stable enough. One way to strengthen a flexible wood floor is by installing a layer of cement backer board on top. Even if the wood floor is sturdy, a waterproof membrane must be laid to protect and insulate the wood. You can use 15-pound building felt (sometimes called "tar paper") for this. Overlap the seams of the felt by at least five inches. Next, lay down metal lath.

Next, lay down metal lath sheets over the building felt. Make sure that the seams of the lath overlap by at least $1/2$ inch. (Metal lath sheets are available at most drywall or masonry-supply stores. They are usually 2 feet wide and 6 to 8 feet long.) Also check to make sure that the sheets lie perfectly flat on the floor. Metal lath can easily be cut to length or shaped to fit an irregular space with ordinary tin snips.

At this point, the mud can be poured. Use a mixture of 50/50 portland cement and fine builder's sand for the mud. (Do not use beach sand as an aggregate with cement.) A good workable mixture of concrete is one that sticks together without crumbling. It is essential to use fine sand, without pebbles, for this mix to ensure that the mud penetrates the spaces within the metal lath while, at the same time, making a smooth top surface with no lumps. The screeding process is often referred to as "striking off the concrete surface."

The 50/50 portland cement is the standard mix for a mud floor. There is, however, another cement product that is formulated for substrate floors. It is called drypack, and it differs from ordinary concrete in that less

water is needed to make the mix. Unlike ordinary concrete, which calls for water to be poured into the mix, thus creating a paste-like consistency, with drypack the water is dribbled into the mix with a sponge. The drypack should not become a paste, but instead should have the consistency of wet beach sand.

The drypack is then shoveled onto the metal lath and smoothed like the traditional 50/50 portland cement mixture. When the floor cures—curing time will be shorter for the drypack floor—it will be as hard and smooth as a 50/50 portland cement floor. Because drypack has less cohesion than an ordinary cement mixture, it cannot be used to smooth walls. It will only crumble and fall away before it has had a chance to harden.

Whether a traditional cement mixture or drypack is used, the smoothing operation is the same. Use a trowel to spread and smooth the cement on the floor. To ensure that the floor is perfectly smooth and flat, finish the surface with a screed. The screed is a long board with flat and true edges (a long metal level can also be used as a screed). It is raked across the surface of the newly poured cement and moved from side to side to smooth and flatten any high spots while pushing excess material into depressions.

ESTABLISHING THE LAYOUT LINES

Before spreading any adhesive, it is essential to establish a starting point where you will begin laying down the tiles **(7–30)**. If the floor is square, the first course can be positioned along one wall provided there will not be any cut border tiles. Usually, it is best to start near the midpoint of the floor. This will ensure that the field is centered and the cut border tiles will end up equally distributed along the walls.

To establish the midpoint of the room, measure the distance between opposite walls and divide that number in half. Transfer that measurement to the floor, and snap a chalk line at that point—making sure that it is parallel to the walls and equidistant between

them. One chalk line should follow the length of the room, and the other will follow the width; they should intersect at the approximate center of the room. Use a framing square to make sure that the intersection between the lines forms a 90-degree angle.

Next, lay the tiles out along the chalk lines, leaving spaces for the grout gaps. This is a dry layout, without any adhesive. It will show how well the actual tiles conform to the paper plan. The gap between the end tiles and the wall should be at least half a tile width **(7–31)**. If it is not, reposition the tiles so the gap will be wider. This can be done by moving the center point or by adjusting the grout space between the tiles.

If any obvious adjustments have been made, the guidelines may have to be reestablished. At this point, you may also want to reposition them so the tiles can be set closer to one wall or near a corner and not directly in the center. This may make it easier to "back

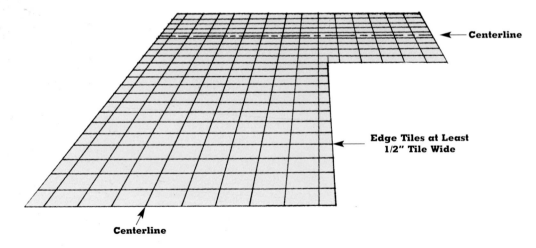

7–30. *Before spreading any adhesive, it is important to establish a starting point for the installation. For small rectangular rooms, drawing two centerlines, one along the length, the other along the width of the room, will be sufficient. Use a framing square to make sure that the lines intersect at right angles. For more complicated rooms, you may have to draw a grid on the floor to ensure a good installation. In an L-shaped room, it helps to divide the room into two sections, establish the centerlines, and connect them. Then draw the grid to plan the installation.*

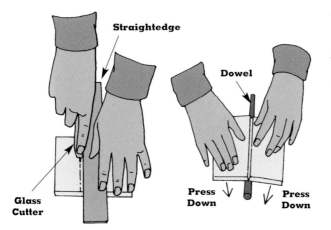

Straightedge

Dowel

Glass Cutter

Press Down   **Press Down**

7–31. In virtually all tile installations, tile-cutting will be necessary to fit the pieces along the edges of the room. The installation should be planned so these edge pieces are at least one-half a tile width. If you only need to cut a few tiles, a glass cutter can be used. Score the tile with the glass cutter; then make the break by placing the tile over a large nail or dowel. Align the tile so the scored line is directly over the dowel, and then press down on the edges of the tile with both hands.

your way out of the room" without having to walk across freshly laid tiles. Use the tiles in the dry layout to pick a point nearer to the wall and snap a new chalk line. Snap another line perpendicular to this one to establish a new intersection.

This method works well for rooms that are rectangular, but some adjustment is needed for L-shaped rooms and for adjoining rooms. This is really not a complicated problem. For the L-shaped room, it helps to first divide the room into two sections and connect the centerlines. Since L-shaped rooms have six walls, not four, it is essential to carefully do a dry layout of the tiles and make sure that the border tiles at any point around the perimeter of the room are not too narrow.

Adjoining rooms can pose a minor problem if they are not the same size, because then the centerlines will be out of alignment. An easy way to correct this is by moving one centerline so it aligns with the one in the other room. In this way, the tiles and the grout lines will align between the two rooms and the final installation will look continuous.

The preceding instructions assume that the tile field will be parallel to the walls. In

contrast to this is the diagonal field **(7–32)**. Here the tiles and grout lines run at a 45-degree angle to the walls. For this layout, it is necessary to snap a second set of working

7–32. An effective use of low-relief tiles introduced into a floor pattern. An additional design nuance is created when the field tiles are laid in a diagonal pattern that contrasts with the border tiles.

lines. Like the first set, these will be perpendicular to each other. They will also intersect at the same point that the initial working lines did. The new lines, however, will bisect the 90-degree angle created by the intersection of the original lines. A protractor or the Pythagorean theorem can be used to set this angle. Once the new lines are snapped in place, follow the same procedures for dry-laying the tiles and making adjustments to the lines.

The working lines are guides to make sure that the tiles are aligned properly. To be effective, they must be visible. Unfortunately, some beginners make the mistake of obscuring them as they spread the adhesive. One way to avoid this problem is by positioning battens along the working lines. These are simply straight 1 × 2 or 1 × 3 boards that are nailed or screwed down to the substrate. The battens serve as a tangible guide that makes it easy to align the tiles perfectly.

At this point, the adhesive can be spread, but before doing this it may be advisable to double check the work. One way to do this is by positioning the layout stick along the lines to see that all the lines are positioned accurately. Another way to verify the accuracy of the work is by laying out the tiles without the adhesive (called a "dry layout") to see how they fit. Admittedly, this can be time-consuming in a large room, but it is an effective way to spot problems and correct them before they become glued in place. This is also an effective way to see whether there are any tiles that need to be changed or repositioned because of their shading or color; this can happen if more than one manufacturing lot is being used.

SPREADING THE ADHESIVE AND LAYING THE TILES

Bring the tools and materials to the working area at least 24 hours prior to the installation. This will allow the tiles and adhesive time to adjust to the temperature and humidity of the room. Before spreading the adhesive over the floor, sweep the floor carefully to remove all grit and dirt; then wipe it with a damp sponge. This damp wipe will ensure that all minute particles of dust and dirt that might adversely affect the bond between the adhesive and the subfloor are picked up.

Mix the adhesive according to the manufacturer's instructions. Spread the adhesive on the floor with the smooth trowel, being careful not to obscure the working lines or pile too much adhesive along the battens. After laying down a generous layer of adhesive, use the toothed trowel (consult the instructions on the adhesive package to find the recommended tooth configuration) to comb it.

It is important to make sure that the adhesive is the right consistency and depth before proceeding too far into the project. One way to do this is by placing a tile down into the adhesive, and then pulling it up again. Examine the back of the tile to see whether the adhesive covers the entire surface. If not, the adhesive may be too viscous. Also, the back of the tile may not have complete coverage if the wrong notched trowel was used to comb the adhesive. A trowel with a fine tooth may make ridges that are too shallow for large tiles. Try recombing the adhesive with another toothed trowel and then test the tile again.

It is sometimes difficult to achieve a smooth and consistent spread of adhesive on tiles that have ridged or patterned backs no matter how the adhesive was combed or its consistency altered. These tiles require a special technique called "buttering." Here a putty knife is used to spread a generous layer of adhesive directly on the back of the tile, the way a slice of bread is buttered (hence the name of the technique). Adhesive must still be spread on the subfloor before the tiles are laid down. Buttering can also be done to raise a tile that is thinner than the others (this is sometimes the case with handmade tiles) or to raise one that sinks below the others on an uneven floor.

All adhesives have a "setup" time (also called "working" or "open" time), after which they will skin over. The tiles must be put down before this occurs; otherwise, the bond between the tiles and adhesive will be a weak one and the tiles will most likely pop up after time. First-time tile setters may have difficulty gauging the setup time for the adhesive. For them, it is best to spread a small amount of adhesive (about a square yard) and see whether this allows enough time to set the tiles precisely. Gradually, they can increase the spread area as they develop proficiency.

Place the tiles by pushing them, one at a time, into the adhesive (7–33). It helps if a twisting motion is applied to the tile as it is set into the adhesive. This will cause it to sink down and it will spread the adhesive across the back of the tile. When setting the tiles, be careful not to slide them against each other. This will cause the adhesive to slide up around the tile edges and fill the grout joints.

Position each tile in place and leave a gap for the grout. The gap width can be judged by eye, or spacers can be fit in between each tile

Twisting Motion

7–33. *Place the tiles in the adhesive by pushing them, one at a time, into the adhesive. It helps if a twisting motion is used on the tile as you push it down. This will cause it to sink and it helps spread the adhesive across the back of the piece.*

that remain in place until you are ready to grout. A temporary spacer can also be used, such as another tile or a thin piece of wood that is pulled out after the tile is in place.

While setting the tiles, pause occasionally to check the work. Use a square and straightedge to make sure the tiles are positioned in a straight line. If they are not, don't panic; simply wiggle the tiles to realign them.

Use the level frequently to make sure the tiles are all on the same plane. Use a beating block and rubber mallet placed across the surface of the tiles to set them into the adhesive. Remember that the beating block may not be effective if the tiles are uneven. Using the block on tiles with a raised pattern across the face may cause them to pop up at the edges. And, of course, the beating block should never be used on thin or delicate tiles—this technique could crack or split the tiles. When in doubt, use your hand to pound the tiles in place.

Tiles that sink below the surface of the adjacent pieces should be picked up and buttered with more adhesive, and then replaced and reset.

At some point, when large areas of the floor have been tiled, it may be necessary to walk across the tiles to work in a corner or near the edge. This can be a problem, because walking on newly set tiles will cause them to shift, sink, or pop up. This can be avoided by placing a sheet of plywood or particleboard down across the tiles—it may be helpful to put thick paper down first to protect the tile faces. The panel will distribute your weight over a large area so you can walk without disturbing individual tiles.

CUTTING TILES FOR THE EDGES

When the field tiles are down, you can work around the edges, that is, near the walls. The field tiles will be whole tiles (tiles that do not need to be cut). With some layouts, it may be possible that a row of tiles mating with a wall will be whole tiles. Along the other walls, however, the tiles will have to be cut to fit.

Either a tile saw or a snap cutter can be used, but first it must be determined where to cut the tile. This may sound like a lot of measuring is in order, but no, there is an easy

trick to this. All that is needed are two whole tiles—both of them clean, that is, without adhesive—and a black marker or a grease pencil.

Call the first tile "A" and place it directly on top of a full-sized tile next to the gap that needs to be filled. Place the second tile, B, on top of tile A; then push it to the side so one edge butts against the wall. Only part of tile B will now be resting on tile A; the other part will span across the gap to be filled. Using the edge of tile B that rests on A as a guide, use the marker to draw a line on the surface of tile A.

This is the exact width of the gap to be filled. However, this does not allow space for the grout. Measure back from this line a distance equal to the width of the grout joint, and make another line parallel to the first. Marking this second line only one grout width away from the first assumes that there is only one joint between the field tiles and the gap tile. The other edge of the gap tile will butt directly against the wall without grout.

This, however, is not a good idea because it does not leave any room for the expansion and contraction of the tile floor. It is better to leave a gap between the tile and the wall and fill it with flexible caulk. When measuring back from the first line (at the edge of tile B), double the distance so it is equal to two grout joints. Press the tile in place, making sure there is a gap between the field tile on one side and the wall on the other. Cut all the necessary tiles. Then spread the adhesive and position the tiles in the gaps around the field perimeter.

APPLYING THE GROUT

Allow at least 24 hours (many manufacturers recommend a minimum of 48 hours) for the adhesive to dry. Clean off any adhesive residue or debris and remove the spacers from between the tiles.

Mix the grout according to the manufacturer's directions. Then use a grout trowel to push the grout into the gaps between the tiles (the technique for applying the grout is covered in more detail in Chapter 6). Wait 15 to 20 minutes for the grout to set; then use a sponge to wipe off the tile surface. Shape the grout joints; then apply a sealer.

Technically this completes the job, but there is another consideration. Tiling a floor generally raises it slightly and the new raised floor may not match the level of the floor in an adjoining room. The only place this will be noticeable, of course, will be at the doorway between the two rooms. Here a transition will have to be made between the two levels. Admittedly, the difference between the two will probably be less than one inch, but still this can often present a tripping hazard **(7–34)**.

An easy way to solve the problem is by installing a threshold (sometimes called a saddle or a transition strip) on the subfloor in the doorway. The bottom of the piece is flat, but the top tapers so it rises from the lower floor level to the higher level of the tiles. The threshold can be positioned before or after the tile job depending upon the layout of the floors and complexity of the tile installation. Still, it is important to plan for the threshold during the layout stage of the tile job.

Tile dealers and home centers may have suitable thresholds to fit your requirements or one can be custom-made to your specifications. Thresholds are available in a variety

7–34. *Mating floors that have different coverings or rise to different levels can present problems. The first is the problem of visual disparity; the second is a problem of bridging the variation in height so as to avoid a tripping problem. Here a wide, hardwood divider solves both problems.*

of materials: the common choices are wood, metal, or stone. Since the new threshold will be higher than the existing one, it will be necessary to remove the door and trim the bottom for clearance.

8

CHAPTER

Tiling Walls

◆

At first glance, it may seem that the technique for tiling a wall is exactly the same as for floor tiling. Think of the wall as a floor, a flat horizontal surface standing on end to become a vertical surface. Indeed, the techniques for tiling wall and floor surfaces are similar, but there are a few significant differences between the two installations.

First, there is the matter of choosing the tile. Obviously, the considerations involved in choosing the color, pattern, and texture of the floor tiles apply to the choice of wall tiles.

The reader is advised to read the chapter on tiling floors to get some understanding of the variables involved. A room, however, has only one floor surface, but it has four wall surfaces. This provides some options that are not available when tiling the floor. You may, for example, elect to surface all four walls with tile, or just one, two, or three. You may also decide to surface the lower half of the wall. This is referred to as wainscoting **(8–2)**. In the bathroom, the tile can be confined to the shower stalls and tub surrounds; or the tiles can be

8–1 (opposite page). *This kind of creative wall installation requires careful planning and meticulous attention to detail.* **(Photo courtesy of Trikeenan Tileworks Inc.)**

8–2. The tiles used in this floor installation serve to visu-ally join two adjacent rooms. The neutral color, along with a basic field pattern, ensures that the floor will not clash with the decorating scheme in either room. The wall tiles rise halfway up the wall. This is referred to as wain-scoting. **(Photo courtesy of Dal–Tile Tile Company)**

8–3. Picture tiles can be combined with solid color tiles to create imaginative designs. When planning any design, choose something that you will be able to live with over time, because it involves a lot of time and work to change the wall if you tire of it. **(Photo courtesy M.E. Tile Company)**

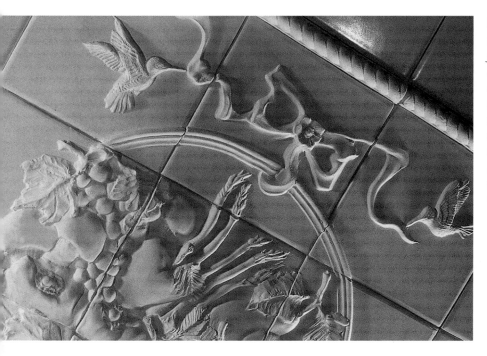

8–4. Some manufacturers offer relief tiles that can be grouped to form a wall sculpture. These tiles are often expensive, but they can be used to add a strong focal point to a plain tile surface. The closeup of this high-relief tile installation shows the fine detail of this partic-ular piece. Tiles like this are beau-tiful to look at, but are difficult to clean. **(Photo courtesy of M.E. Tile Company)**

extended onto one of the adjacent walls to give the room a more unified look. The tiles can also be repeated in subtle ways to create accents within the room. For example, a window, door, or mounted mirror can be framed with a row of tiles and the surrounding wall left as a flat, untiled surface.

One wall can be chosen as a focal point and tiled with a dramatic pattern while the adjacent walls are kept in a monochromatic scheme. Picture or mural tiles can be used as patterns **(8–3)**. These are individual tiles that have parts of a picture imprinted on their surface. When the tiles are joined together, they form a mural that adds visual interest to an otherwise plain wall.

An interesting variation to the mural idea incorporates a group of raised tiles to form a low-relief sculpture. Specialty tile manufacturers and individual craftsmen make tile sculptures that can be mounted on a wall surface to create a dramatic counterpoint to an otherwise commonplace tiled surface **(8–4)**.

Some tile manufacturers offer tiles in trompe l'oeil patterns **(refer to 8-1)**, designs of interior architectural elements executed in realistic perspective that create the illusion of columns, elaborate moldings, or pilasters. Used with imagination, they can transform an ordinary flat wall into an intricate and interesting design that suggests the interior of a Renaissance study or Victorian parlor.

Different colors can be used for different walls. This may be done as an effort to reshape a room. If, for example, it is a long narrow room, dark tiles can be put on the end walls. This will make those walls look closer together and create the illusion of a room that is not as long. Of course, this only works if both ends

of the room can be seen at the same time.

The textural choices for floor tiles are limited by function. It is not a good idea to choose floor tiles that have deep or delicate textures because they could be worn away with heavy traffic or could create a tripping hazard. Then, too, smooth tiles could be slippery. This is not a problem with wall tiles. Here a fantasy for intricate and unusual textures can be indulged without having to worry about creating a potential safety hazard.

CHECKING THE WALLS

The first thing to do before doing a layout or buying any tiles is to examine the walls with a straightedge, framing square, level, and plumb bob to determine how square and true they are. It is possible to install the tiles if the walls have minor deviations, but walls that are out of square will need a border row of tiles cut at acute angles to fit against the adjacent walls. It is best then to be fully aware of these problems before beginning.

Checking the accuracy of the walls is important because wall distortions will become obvious and even exaggerated when the tiles are in place. This is because the geometric tile patterns and grout lines will look wavy and out of alignment if the walls are not true.

Use the plumb bob and a chalk line to see if the walls are square **(8–5)**. Suspend the plumb bob from the top of the wall a few inches from the corner where the walls meet. Snap a chalk line along the plumb line. Then measure the distance from the corner to the line at the top, center, and bottom. These measurements will reveal whether the walls are square with each other, and if not, how severe the anomaly is.

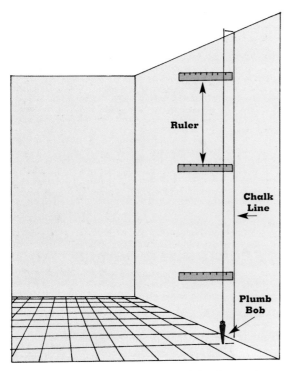

8–5. *Check the walls with a plumb bob to be sure that they are perfectly flat. Suspend the plumb bob from the top of the wall and measure the distance from the cord to the wall at several points. The measurement between the cord and wall should be consistent at the top, middle, and bottom of the wall.*

If the wall is less than ¹/₈ inch out of plumb, there will be no need to cut the tiles because the grout joint can be adjusted to fill this minor gap. A more serious deviation from plumb may require cutting the border tiles to fit or removing the wallboard and replacing it with new backing that is shimmed to make it square.

Check to see that the walls are square with the ceiling. Draw a horizontal line across the wall a few inches below the ceiling and then take measurements to see if the distance from the line to the ceiling is consistent at each checkpoint. Use a long level to draw the horizontal line. Use the same technique to check the walls against the floor.

Next, check to see that the walls meet at a 90-degree angle by placing the framing square in the corner. Rarely will the corners form a perfect right angle; there is bound to be some slight variation. This presents no problem as long as the angle is not too open.

Finally, check to see that the walls are perfectly flat. Hold a long straightedge against the wall to see whether there are any obvious depressions or bumps along the surface of the wall. Sometimes it helps to hold a flashlight under the level while peering over the top. Depressions or gaps will be obvious when the light shines past the straightedge. The best way to correct walls that are not flat and smooth is by installing new wallboard or cement backer board over the old wall.

PLANNING THE LAYOUT

A good layout is important in any tiling job, because there will be few surfaces that are the exact width and height of a combination of whole tiles. In most cases, some tiles will have to be cut to fit along a border. Planning where these cut tiles will appear can make the difference between a pleasing design pattern that appears centered on the wall or a design that looks slightly askew. As with the floor pattern, the way to create a centered design is to position the tiles so opposite borders have tiles of the same width. In a few instances, it may be possible to adjust the grout width to space the tiles out to the borders so there is no need to cut tiles.

While laying out a tile job for walls is similar to that for a floor installation, wall installations will present some problems that do not exist in floor installations. Wall surfaces are interrupted by door or window openings . The tile pattern will have to fit around these openings **(8–6)**. Often this will necessitate cutting more tiles for the border areas.

If possible, cut the tiles that border on either side of the door or window opening to the same width. This will make the opening appear to be centered in the pattern. While this sounds easy enough, it becomes tricky, because those border tiles and the tiles adjacent to them on either side of the window must also align with those in the courses below. The best way to approach this task is by first planning a full row of base tiles and then building up from there to the window, making adjustments while working up.

As might be suspected, there will be times when a compromise is required when doing the layout. For example, border tiles of different widths might have to be put at opposite ends of a wall in order to create a centered window pattern. Remember, the plan can be adjusted and modified as often as needed until it is just right.

Often the bottom of a window or the top of a window or door will not line up with the rows of tiles; the space between the bottom of the window and the next row of tiles will be less than a tile width. Here you will have to cut across the tiles so they fit the gap between the window and the row of tiles.

The corners may present an additional problem if there is a gap of less than a whole tile between the edge of the window as well as the bottom with the nearest row. This may require a compound cut—one cut across the tile and one cut down, forming a right-angle cutout—to create a notch so the tile fits around the corner of the door or window frame. If this proves

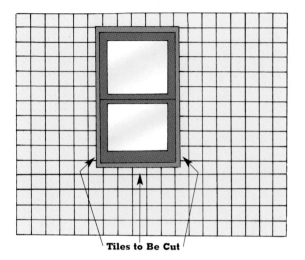

Tiles to Be Cut

8–6. *While laying out a tile job for walls is similar to that for a floor installation, wall installations will present some problems that do not exist in floor installations. Wall surfaces are interrupted by door or window openings. Here the tile installation will have to be fit around these openings. If the tiles around the door and/or window must be cut, try to plan the installation so the tiles on the sides will be cut to the same width.*

to be too difficult, wait until the installation and then bring all the corner tiles to the local tile supplier. Usually he/she will make the necessary cuts for a nominal fee.

As an alternative, the tile can be cut into two pieces. One cut is made across a tile, cutting it in two. Another cut is made on the top piece of the newly cut tile. (This assumes the tile will fit in a lower corner. If the tile is to fit on one of the top corners, then the second cut will be on the bottom piece of the newly cut tile.) With these cuts, two smaller tiles are created (actually there will be three pieces, but the corner piece will be discarded), both rectangular in shape, that fit around the corners of the window or door. It may seem premature to consider cutting tiles while in the layout stage, but often a little adjustment at this time can eliminate or at least minimize extensive cutting.

Another factor to consider in a wall layout is the possible problem of continuing the pattern from one wall onto an adjoining wall. Decisions have to be made regarding whether to use cut tiles in the corners or whole tiles, and then how to best fit the tiles across the entire surface. This is not a serious problem. In most cases if there is a cut tile on the edge of one wall, it is advisable to meet it with a cut tile of the same width on the adjacent wall.

ESTIMATING THE AMOUNT OF MATERIAL NEEDED

The procedure for estimating the amount of tile, adhesive, and grout needed for the walls is the same as for floors, with one difference. To estimate the amount of material to cover any surface, the square footage of that surface is needed. This is obtained by measuring the width and height of the surface and then multiplying the two figures.

This is straightforward enough, but with a wall surface the calculations become slightly more complicated because the wall usually has openings—windows, doors, a fireplace, mounted cabinets, etc.—that will not be covered with tile. If the area for these fixtures is not subtracted, there will be more tile, adhesive, and grout (and a larger bill) than needed.

There are two ways to calculate wall area. For the first, measure the width and height of the wall and multiply the two. This will give the total wall area. Next, measure the width and height of every door, window, or fixture on the wall, and calculate the respective area of each. Add these total areas together and then subtract the figure from the total wall area.

The second method requires that the wall be treated as a combination of individual parts to be joined together. To calculate wall area with this method, divide the entire wall into separate rectangles that surround all openings and fixtures on the surface. Measure the dimensions of each rectangle, multiply to find the area, and then add the figures to calculate the total area.

Since tile is usually sold by the square foot, calculate how much tile is needed to cover the wall and then add 10 percent to cover breakage. Adhesive coverage is best figured by looking at the label on the adhesive package. This will give guidelines for the amount of adhesive needed for the various areas.

The amount of grout needed will depend on the number of tiles used and the width of the grout joints. Typical grout widths for wall tiles are between $1/8$ and $3/16$ inch. Again, package labels will offer guidelines for the amount of grout needed.

It is a good idea to go over the figures with the local tile supplier so he can double-check them for accuracy and to be sure that enough materials will be ordered. It is better to have too much than not enough. In most cases, the tile dealer will take back any unopened packages for a refund.

PRELIMINARY ROOM PREPARATION

Before the installation can begin, all the fixtures must be removed from the walls. Next, the walls should be inspected for defects. These must be repaired or else the tiles will not adhere properly to the walls.

Before doing anything, however, take the time to protect the floor in the room being

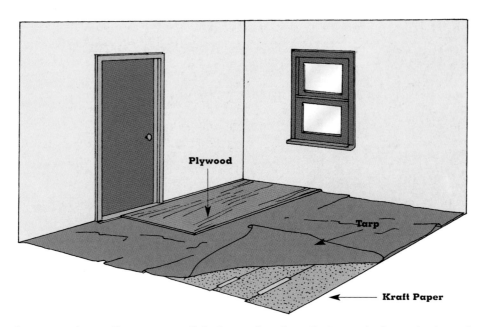

8–7. *Before starting the installation, remove all the fixtures from the walls. Protect the floor with a layer of waterproof kraft paper. Place a heavy-duty drop cloth on top of the paper. As an added protection, lay a thin panel of plywood or particleboard down. The panel will protect the floor from damage that might occur when a tool or tile is dropped.*

worked on and adjacent floors in the hallway or rooms leading to the workroom **(8–7)**. Cover the entire floor with a layer of waterproof kraft paper. Place a heavy-duty drop cloth on top of the kraft paper. As an added barrier to protect the floor from dropped tools or tiles, place a sheet of thin plywood or particleboard on the floor in the area that is being worked on. Move the board around while working on other walls.

This should be enough if the walls are in good condition, but if any power sanding has to be done, cover all heating and cooling registers with heavy plastic film and duct tape. Use heavy plastic film to make a movable "curtain" over the entry doorway. This will help to contain the dust and prevent it from spreading throughout the house. Place old doormats or towels on the floor on both sides of the doorway. Use these to wipe your feet

and to avoid tracking dust while walking from the work site.

Now remove all the wall hangings, such as pictures and hangers, drapery and curtain rods, and towel bars. Then remove all the switch plates and outlet covers and wall-mounted light fixtures.

Remove any trim molding around the walls, doors, and windows **(8–8)**. Insert a pry bar about a foot from one end of the molding. Place a wide-blade taping knife between the pry bar and the wall to prevent the bar from damaging the wall as you gently pry the molding away. If you are planning to replace the molding after the tiling is complete, remove the nails and fill the nail holes with wood filler.

On molding that proves stubborn and difficult to pry off, use a hammer and nail set to drive the nails through the molding into

8–8. *Remove all the trim molding from around the doors and windows. Use a pry bar to pull the molding away from the wall. Insert it about a foot from one end of the molding; then place a wide taping knife under the pry bar to protect the wall. Carefully pry the molding away, being careful not to damage or split the wood.*

the wall. When the nails are completely through, pry the molding away and pull the nails from the wall by gripping the protruding heads.

If the floor covering is of resilient flooring, the base molding may be made of vinyl. Vinyl base molding is held in place with adhesive. It is possible to break the adhesive bond and release the molding by pushing a wide-blade taping knife between the base and the wall and then prying outward. Use a portable hair dryer (not a torch) to soften unyielding adhesive bond.

REMOVING BATHROOM FIXTURES

In the bathroom, it may be possible to cut tiles to fit around the sink and toilet, but this

might leave gaps if the fixtures are replaced later on. It is better to remove the lavatory and toilet and tile the entire wall surface. Before attempting this, shut off the water to each fixture by closing the shutoff valves projecting from the walls. If there are no shutoff valves, close the main valve to the house water supply. Of course, this will necessitate shutting off the household water supply.

If you are working in an empty house, this will not be a problem, but if the house is occupied the water cannot be left off for very long. However, the supply pipes can be closed by installing caps on their ends. Then the water can be turned on again. After the tiling is completed, it is advisable to consider installing shutoff valves before replacing the fixtures.

Once the water is shut off, start removing the fixtures. To remove the lavatory **(8–9)**, first unloosen the compression nuts that con-

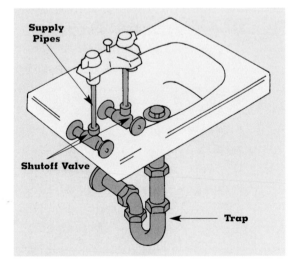

8–9. *In the bathroom, it will be easier to install tiles on the wall if the lavatory is removed. Be sure to shut off the water to the fixture before disconnecting any pipes. Unloosen the compression nuts that connect the supply pipes to the shutoff valves. Then unloosen the compression nuts on the drainpipe. At this point, the pipes can be pulled apart and the sink removed.*

nect the supply pipes to the shutoff valves. Use an adjustable wrench for this, but first wrap the wrench jaws with masking tape to protect the finish on the nuts.

Now use channel-lock pliers or a basin wrench to turn the coupling nuts so the drain can be disconnected under the basin. Check to see if the sink has a pop-up stopper. Usually the linkage for the stopper has a vertical rod that runs from the fixture and joins a horizontal rod that hooks into the stopper in the drainpipe. With this arrangement, there is no need to remove the linkage; it will remain self-contained and stay attached to the sink when it is removed. But be careful not to bump the linkage when removing the sink; this could bend the rods.

When the supply pipes, drainpipe, and stopper linkage have been disconnected, the sink can be removed. A sink that is wall-mounted usually is held in place with hooks that slide into recesses in a wall bracket. To remove the sink, simply lift it off the bracket. Be aware that some sinks can be heavy. Rather than tax your strength, enlist the aid of a helper to lift the sink off the bracket.

If the sink is mounted in a vanity cabinet, the cabinet and sink can be removed as one piece. The vanity may be attached to the wall or floor with angle brackets. If so, the brackets must be removed—usually these are held with wood screws—before the vanity can be pulled away.

It may not be necessary to remove the toilet to tile the walls, but some bathrooms are small and in some cases the toilet may be so close to the wall that it will be difficult to work properly. In these instances, it may be better to take the time to remove the toilet so there is enough clearance to do the tile installation properly. For the toilet removal procedure, see the chapter on tiling floors.

CHECKING AND PREPARING A WALLBOARD SURFACE

Most modern homes have walls made of wallboard (also called "drywall"). Wallboard provides a good surface for tile provided it is flat, smooth, and firm. Inspect the wallboard for dents, cracks, holes, and loose nails. These must be repaired before applying the tile **(8–10)**. Fortunately, wallboard damage is easy to repair. The following tools are needed: a 6-inch taping or putty knife, an 6-inch joint knife, a utility knife, a compass or a wallboard saw, a metal straightedge, sandpaper, and a dust mask.

Some compound is needed for sealing cracks and patching dents. The variety and nomenclature of these compounds may be a little confusing at first. There's patching plaster, spackling compound, joint taping com-

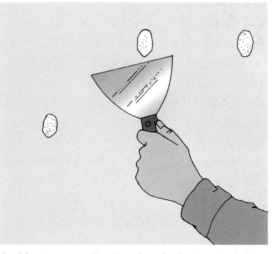

8–10. *Examine all wall surfaces for dents, cracks, holes, and loose nails. These defects must be repaired before installing the tiles. Use spackling compound to fill and cover these defects. Apply the compound with a wide taping knife. When the compound dries, sand it smooth.*

pound, joint topping compound, and all-purpose joint compound. *Patching plaster* dries quickly, but is difficult to sand. It also requires mixing. It's not a good choice for general repair. *Spackling compound* is designed to fill cracks and dents in wallboard. It dries faster, with less shrinkage, than joint compound but is more difficult to sand smooth. *Taping compounds* are used to fill in joints and apply tape. *Topping compounds* are used for second and third layers over the tape. *All-purpose joint compound* combines the advantages of taping and topping compounds. It takes longer to dry than spackling compound, but is easier to sand. If you have the time and patience to make the repair, then all-purpose joint compound is the best choice.

The studs in newly constructed houses can sometimes warp or shrink. This causes the nails to loosen and pop out. If possible, pull the nails out and drive new nails an inch away from the original ones. Hammer each new nail slightly below the surface of the wallboard, creating a dimple; but do not tear the paper surface of the panel. Use a six-inch taping knife to fill the dimple with patching compound. Let the compound dry, and then apply a second coat. When it dries, sand it smooth (wear a dust mask) and then prime and paint it.

An even better remedy for popped nails is to remove and replace them with drywall screws. These have better gripping power than nails and are less likely to pop out over time.

Sometimes the paper tape covering the panel joints works loose and lifts up. When this happens, cut the tape at the top and bottom of the section, and then peel off the loose tape. Next, apply a generous coat of joint com-

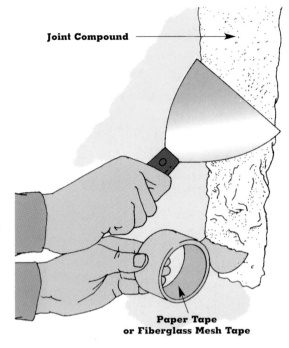

Joint Compound

Paper Tape or Fiberglass Mesh Tape

8–11. *Cover open seams or wide cracks with paper or fiberglass. First cut the tape to length; then apply a generous coat of joint compound to the crack. Embed the tape in the wet compound and smooth the area with the taping knife. Allow the compound to dry; then apply a second coat. After the second coat dries, apply a third coat.*

pound over the area. Cut a strip of paper tape to the length of the old piece and embed it in the compound. Using the taping knife, make a pass over the tape. This should smooth the joint and remove excess compound. Allow this to dry; then apply a second, thin coat, covering the tape. Let this dry and apply a third coat with an 8-inch joint knife, drawing the compound smooth and feathering the edges so they blend into the surrounding wall.

Filling a small dent in wallboard is essentially the same as filling a nail dimple. Fill the dent with patching compound and then smooth the area with the taping knife. When the area is dry, apply a second coat by drawing the taping knife across the patch at right angles to the first pass. This crisscross technique will ensure that the final coat is smooth.

The same dent-filling technique can be used to repair small holes, but holes larger than 2 inches require a more substantial patch **(8–11)**. First use a compass or wallboard saw to shape the hole into a neat rectangle. Before making these cuts, check to make sure that there are no pipes or wires behind the wall.

Cut a wallboard patch about 2 inches larger than the hole on each side (if the hole is 2 X 2 inches, the patch will be 6 X 6 inches). Place the patch face down on a table and with a utility knife cut through the paper backing into the plaster core. Do not cut completely through the plaster or the paper on the face side. Snap and peel off the plaster pieces from the borders. Leave the center rectangle attached to the face paper so there is a solid rectangular core of plaster surrounded by a two-inch-wide paper border.

Smear a generous amount of joint compound on the paper border and also around the edges of the hole in the wall. Position the patch so that the center block fits into the opening of the damaged area. The border flaps will then overlap the surrounding wall. Go over the patch with the six-inch taping knife and squeeze the excess joint compound from around the edges. Allow the patch 24 hours to dry before applying a second coat of compound. Apply the second coat on top of the patch and around the border flaps. Feather this coat so that it blends in smoothly with the surrounding walls. Apply a final thin coat when the second coat is dry. Sand this smooth, and then prime and paint.

For very large holes and damaged areas, enlarge the hole by cutting it back to the center of the nearest studs **(8–12)**. Since the studs are usually 16 inches apart center to center, the patch will be 16 inches wide. Trim the damaged area with a utility knife to make a rectangular opening. Cut a patch from wallboard to fit the opening, and then nail or screw it to the studs. Tape the joints, and then spread a thin layer of compound over the repaired area, feathering the edges. When it is dry, sand the patch smooth; then prime and paint.

An easy way to check the rigidity of a wallboard surface is by pressing against it, midway between the studs, with your hand. If the wall flexes, then it is too weak to support

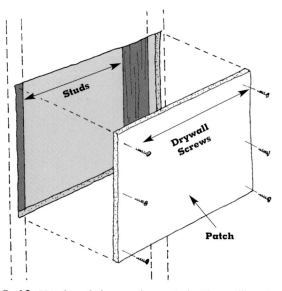

8–12. *Very large holes must be repaired with a wallboard patch. First enlarge the hole by cutting it back to the center of the nearest studs. Since most studs are usually 16 inches apart center to center, the patch will have to be at least 16 inches wide. Cut the patch to fit the new opening; then fit it into the opening and fasten it with either nails or wallboard screws. Tape the joints; then spread a thin layer of compound over the entire area, feathering the edges to the surrounding areas. When the compound is dry, sand the patch smooth; then prime and paint it.*

the weight of a tiled wall and it must be reinforced.

USING BACKER BOARD TO REINFORCE A WEAK WALL

The best way to reinforce a weak wall is to cover it with cement backer board (referred to in the tiling trade as cementitious backer units, and abbreviated CBU). This is more rigid than ordinary wallboard and it will provide good support for the tile. Measure and mark the CBU and then cut it to size. A carbide-tipped scriber can be used to score the board along the lines. Press down firmly and use a straightedge for accuracy. Make several passes to create a groove about $1/16$ inch deep. Turn the board over and do the same on the other side, making sure that both grooves align with each other. Now grab one end of the board and gently pull up to snap it in two. The resulting break should be reasonably straight. It should be smoothed by rubbing the edge with a masonry rubbing stone (available at tile dealers).

If the installation is large and a number of panels have to be cut, you may want to rent a power hand grinder fitted with a dry-cutting diamond wheel. This will make a quick cut and leave a smooth edge on the board. Another option is to rent a reciprocating saw fitted with a carbide-tipped blade design for cutting hard materials.

For most walls, the board only has to be cut to the correct dimensions, but for walls with supply pipes projecting, holes also have to be drilled for the plumbing. First measure the location of the existing pipes, and then transfer the measurements to the board. Take the time to do this accurately or there will be a lot of unnecessary holes and wasted CBU.

Professionals can "punch" a hole in backer board by striking it sharply with a hammer, but this takes practice. It is easier for the novice to chuck a carbide-tipped hole saw into an electric drill and bore the holes.

The cut board can be nailed to the wall studs with galvanized roofing nails. Special CBU screws can also be bought and driven with a power screwdriver. Do not use ordinary drywall nails or screws if doing an installation for a wet area, like the bathroom. They are not corrosion-resistant.

CHECKING AND PREPARING WALLS MADE OF PLASTER

Older homes usually have plaster walls. Plaster provides a good tile surface, provided that it is in good repair and that it does not have a high lime content. How can you determine the lime content of the plaster? There is a simple test that can be performed with an ordinary screwdriver. Poke the plaster in a few places with the tip of the screwdriver. If the plaster remains hard and does not crumble, then it is suitable as a substrate for tiling. Soft and crumbling plaster usually has a high lime content and will not hold the weight of a tile wall. It should be replaced.

Common defects occurring in a plaster wall are cracks (both hairline and wide cracks) and holes. Hairline cracks are normal in plaster surfaces and are no cause for concern. They should be filled before tiling the wall. First enlarge them with the point of a can opener or a chisel and undercut the crack to provide a key for the new patching compound **(8–13)**. Remove any plaster dust with a stiff-bristled brush, and then fill the crack with spackling compound.

Small holes can be filled with joint compound. Larger ones (more than five inches in diameter) should be cut to the nearest studs and then fitted with a wallboard patch. Before fitting the new patch, secure the plaster around the hole with plaster washers. Screw the patch to the nearby studs with drywall screws. Complete the job by taping around the joint between the patch and the plaster. Cover the tape with joint compound.

Another kind of crack common to plaster walls is the cyclical crack. These cracks open and close as the humidity changes. It's best to apply fiberglass tape in a bed of joint compound over the crack. When this dries, apply more compound, feathering the edges, to conceal the tape.

A larger and more serious crack is the structural crack. These cracks open up when

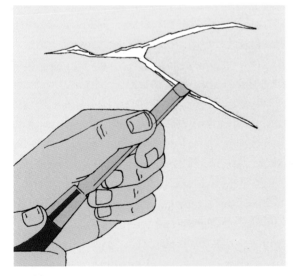

8–13. *The most common defect in plaster walls is cracking. The cracks should be enlarged with a chisel or can opener. The cracks should be undercut to provide a key for the new patching compound. Remove any plaster dust with a stiff-bristled brush; then fill the crack with spackling compound.*

the structural members that support the wall or the entire house settle and shift. Those that occur in the early life (the first five years) of a house are usually stable. They can be filled and taped over. If the crack suddenly starts to enlarge or if one develops in a long-standing house, there may be an active structural problem present. In this case, consult an architect or structural engineer before proceeding.

A more serious problem occurs when the plaster has broken away from the underlying lath and is bulging outward. Plaster that has sagged away from the lath can sometimes be saved with plaster washers, sometimes called "ceiling buttons." These are small discs of sheet metal with a hole in the center. The hole accepts a flat-head wood screw that is driven through the plaster into the lath base. The disc grips the surface of the plaster and prevents it from splitting. Conceal these with joint compound.

Plaster washers may prevent the plaster from splitting, but they are not an ideal solution, because sagging plaster is a sign that the plaster surface is old and weak. The ideal solution is to remove the plaster and lath and then recover the studs with cement backer board.

Wallboard or plaster walls should be fitted with a waterproof membrane (see Chapter 5) if tile will be installed in a wet environment, that is, the bathroom or shower.

CHECKING AND PREPARING WALLS WITH PAINT, WALLPAPER, PANELS, OR WAINSCOTING

Tile can be applied to a painted surface provided the paint is firmly bonded to the wall surface. Loose or peeling paint should be removed. A high-gloss paint surface may not offer enough "tooth" for the tile adhesive; remove the gloss and roughen the surface with sandpaper. Do not attempt to install tiles over a wallpapered surface. Even if the paper seems firmly attached to the wall, the weight of the tiles will eventually cause it to loosen and break free.

Tile should never be applied to a paneled wall or to wainscoting. These surfaces do not make good backing for tiles because they contract and expand with humidity fluctuations and the tile surface will either pop off or crack.

PREPARING MASONRY SURFACES

Freshly poured concrete needs to cure properly before tile can be installed. Allow at least a month for this. If the walls are firm and dry, tile can be installed. Check first, however, to make sure that the surface is indeed dry. Surface moisture will prevent the tile adhesive from bonding. It is caused by groundwater seeping through the porous concrete or from condensation of ambient humidity.

Surface water caused by groundwater is a serious problem, and may require grading the ground surrounding the house or installing a drainage system around the foundation. (In mild cases, it may be possible to seal the wall with a waterproofing paint, but this is taking the chance that the groundwater will not significantly increase.) Moisture caused by condensation is less serious and can be corrected with dehumidifiers and exhaust fans.

If water beads are detected on the walls, how can you determine whether they are coming through the walls or are the result of ambient humidity? There is a simple test for this. First, dry the wall; then tape a piece of aluminum foil about a foot square onto the wall with duct tape. Wait a few days, and then examine the foil. If the moisture has collected on the outside of the patch, that is, the side toward the interior of the room, then it is the result of condensation. If, however, the moisture is on the wall side, then it is caused by water seeping through the wall. This problem must be corrected before installing the tile.

Even if the wall is dry, it may contain efflorescence. This is the deposit of salts and minerals that show up on the surface as white crystals. The salts and minerals emerging through the walls are in solution. As the water evaporates, the crystals are left behind. Efflorescence is not a problem in itself. It can be washed off with a stiff brush, water, and a detergent. This, however, will only relieve the symptoms of the problem. Unless adequate measures are taken, the moisture will continue to seep through the wall and the efflorescence will continue to accumulate.

Even if the wall is reasonably dry, it should be cleaned to remove dirt, dust, grit, or any substance that could interfere with a good adhesive bond. Wash the wall thoroughly with a stiff brush and a mild detergent. Avoid using harsh chemical cleaners or detergents. They can leave a residue on the concrete that will affect the tile adhesive.

Cracks and holes in concrete should be filled with patching cement. It is best to "key" the hole or crack by undercutting it with a cold chisel (be sure to wear goggles and heavy-duty gloves while chiseling). The object in keying is to cut the base of the hole so it is wider than the opening. When the concrete patch dries, it will be wedged into the opening. Allow time for the patch to cure before installing the tiles.

PREPARING A WALL COVERED WITH CERAMIC TILE

Fresh tile can be applied directly to an existing tile surface provided the tile is securely fastened to the wall. One or two loose tiles is not usually cause for concern. They can be scraped clean and remounted. A number of loose or missing tiles is an indication that there is a problem with the adhesive or with the underlying substrate.

Loose tiles may be caused by a poor adhesive bond—either the adhesive was of an inferior grade or it wasn't properly applied. If the majority of the wall tiles are loose, it is best to remove them all and then prepare the surface for a new installation.

If the underlying substrate is at fault, the problem must be corrected before the installation can continue; otherwise, the problem will reoccur. Finding the source of the problem usually requires removing all or most of the loose tiles, scraping off the adhesive, and then monitoring the wall for a few days or a week to see if it remains stable.

If the existing tiles are solid, they must first be cleaned to remove dirt, soap scum, and wax that might be accumulated on the surface. Then they must be rubbed with a Carborundum stone to roughen the surface and remove the glazing. Roughening the surface will provide the necessary "tooth" so the adhesive can grip and bond with the existing tile surface. This task can be accomplished by

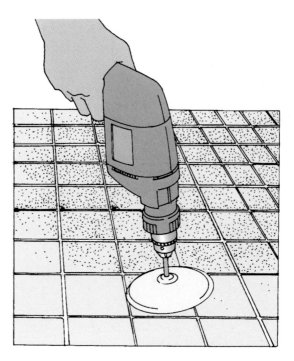

8–14. *It is necessary to roughen the surface to remove the tile glaze and create a "tooth" for the new adhesive. Roughening can be accomplished with a handheld Carborundum stone. This method is slow and tedious, however. For large surfaces, it may be better to use an electric drill fitted with an abrasive wheel.*

hand, but it will be less tedious with an electric sander **(8–14)**. After sanding, wash the surface to remove any loose tile dust.

At this point the tile installation can begin, but first consider the configuration of the existing tiles. If just the existing tile surface will be covered, then proceed. However, suppose the tiles only extend halfway up the wall like wainscoting and the plan is to cover the entire wall from top to bottom. Then the new tile surface will be on two levels: the raised level of the existing tile surface and the lower level of the wall above.

If a smooth, continuous surface on one level is desired, then the wall surface (that part without tiles) has to be raised to match the tile wainscoting below. An easy way to do this is by covering the wall with a layer of $1/4$-inch backer board.

INSTALLING THE TILES

Some manufacturers recommend priming the wall surface before applying their adhesive. Usually the package will offer recommendations for primers. Most primers can be applied with either a brush or a roller.

The procedures for installing wall tiles are basically the same as for installing floor tiles, with one major difference: Gravity has a greater effect on a wall installation. In other words, gravity will start to pull on the tiles and cause them to sag down the wall before the adhesive has time to set. Of course, gravity cannot be eliminated, but precautions can be taken to minimize its effect. Start by laying the bottom row of tiles first, and then work up. In this way, the lower tiles will support the course above them. If heavy tiles are being installed, a batten board can be attached to the wall first to provide a stable support for the tiles.

Before applying the adhesive, establish the working lines. Start with the vertical working line. It should be centered on the wall. Measure the width of the wall, divide that number in half, and use that number to measure and mark the center of the wall.

Use a layout pole (a straight, narrow, measuring stick marked in increments of the individual tile widths and the grout joints in between each tile) to mark off tile and grout increments from the center point to one wall. If the last tile (that is, the one that butts the adjacent wall) is at least one-half a tile width or greater, the center point can be used to establish the vertical working line. If the end tile will be less than one-half tile wide, move the center point away from the wall. This will make the end tiles wider. Once a working center point has been established, use a spirit level to draw a vertical line through the point to the top and bottom of the wall.

Next, establish a horizontal line at the base of the wall. This is not difficult if the floor is perfectly horizontal and level, but most floors dip slightly and imperfections, no matter how minor, could affect the tile layout. To check the floor surface and establish a working line, use the level to draw a perfectly horizontal line across the wall a few inches above the floor. If you are planning to tile the adjacent walls, then use the level to extend this line around to those surfaces also. Measure down from this line at strategic points to the floor surface. The lowest part of the floor will be at the point where this measurement is the greatest, and this will be the starting point for establishing the horizontal working line.

Place a full tile on the floor at this point and place a mark along the top edge. Use this mark to establish a new horizontal working line across the wall and onto the adjacent walls. This new line will be the base line for the first course of tiles. Well, maybe not—there are two conditions that require further adjustment.

Establishing the starting line one tile width above the floor presumes that the wall tiles will come right down to the floor level—as indeed most wall tile installations do—but suppose the floor will be tiled? If the perimeter of the floor field will have cove base tiles, then these will affect the wall layout because cove tiles bend up from the floor a short length onto the wall. This factor has to be taken into consideration by installing the wall tiles to allow sufficient clearance for the cove tiles.

Fortunately, this is not difficult. Before placing the temporary wall tile at the low floor point, position a few cove tiles there. Then put the wall tile on the top edge of the cove tile and mark the top edge to establish a mark for the starting line.

Other factors that may affect the wall layout are window placements and counter installations. If the wall has a window or other opening, adjust the layout so there is a full row of tiles directly beneath the windowsill. It is really no problem to adjust the layout if you mark for a row of tiles under the sill and then use the layout stick to adjust for the course below.

If the wall wraps around a counter, the finished installation will look better if there is a full row of tiles along the countertop. Establish the first horizontal line of tiles above the countertop and then project a line onto the adjacent wall. Use the layout stick to measure down to the base of the wall and establish a starting line.

When you get down to the base of the wall, determine whether the first course will be less than one tile in height. Rather than cut a number of very narrow tiles to make up this course, it is better to install two rows of wider-cut tiles to make up the bottom courses.

CHOOSING AND PLANNING FOR THE ACCESSORIES

Finally plan for any accessories that may be mounted on the walls. These include such items as a ceramic soap dish, a towel bar, or a grab bar. Proper placement of these functional and seemingly insignificant items is what distinguishes a good-looking installation from a run-of-the-mill job.

The first step is, of course, to choose the right accessories for the installation. There are two approaches to choosing accessories. The first assumes that any accessory is purely functional, and, as such, should be placed where it will be accessible but unobtrusive so it doesn't detract from the effect of the installation.

The second approach is just the opposite. With this school of thought, the accessories are chosen for their aesthetic appeal as well as function. Proper placement then depends as much on using the pieces to complement and enhance the overall design of the installation as on positioning each piece where it will be readily accessible. This approach has become increasingly more popular in recent years because a number of manufacturers have introduced accessory lines in a wide range of colors and styles. There are also companies that offer custom-made accessories for the home owner who wants a truly unique tile installation. Most of these items cost more than the traditional pieces, however, and the home owner is apt to add to the cost of the tile installation with this approach.

When it comes to choosing accessories, there is still a third possibility—not choosing them at all. In other words, eliminating the need for ceramic accessories altogether. For example, shelves or ledges can be built into the wall to hold soap or towels. Or a small cabinet can be placed near the sink or tub to hold towels. For soap, a ceramic or metal bowl can be placed on a small stool that is positioned by the tub. Instead of towel bars, hooks can be installed on the walls. Strictly speaking, this approach doesn't really eliminate the accessories but instead trades less-conspicuous and less-conventional items for the pieces that we normally expect to see in the bathroom.

The accessories should be positioned so they line up with the horizontal grout lines of the surrounding field tiles. Many accessories come in dimensions that are multiples of standard tile sizes. Thus they can fit into the field pattern without the necessity of cutting the adjacent tiles. These pieces will be installed after all the field tiles are in place, so it is necessary to plot their location and leave an opening for them.

Bear in mind that not all accessories will be cemented to the wall. Some are mounted with screw-through holes drilled in the tiles. For these accessories, it is not necessary to leave an opening in the field.

THE TILING SEQUENCE

Once the layout is fully conceived, the tiling sequence can be established. It may seem that the most logical installation sequence is to set the tiles in successive horizontal courses. Indeed this is the simplest method, but it may not be the best, because the final installation will look askew if the walls are even slightly out of plumb. It is best to start the first course from the center and work toward the adjacent walls. At the wall, work from the corner up the wall and toward the center.

At this point, the adhesive can be applied and the tiles set in place. Mix the adhesive according to the package directions and spread it with a trowel. Consult the package for recommendations as to the suitable notched-trowel size that is recommended by the manufacturer. Also check to see whether the manufacturer recommends a specific spreading pattern for the adhesive—some adhesives are spread in overlapping arcs, while others are spread at an angle to the courses.

Do not apply more adhesive than can be covered with tile before the adhesive sets up or skins over. It is best to spread the adhesive in a small area so you can judge how much tile can be set in the working or "open" time of the adhesive. As you progress in the installation and gain a greater appreciation for the properties of the materials, you can spread more or less adhesive.

Press the tiles into the fresh adhesive with a slight twisting movement. This will spread the adhesive on the tile back and help seat it firmly. Do not, however, slide the tiles. This action will push excess adhesive onto the tile edges and clog the grout joints. If excessive adhesive is accumulating around the edges of a tile, scrape it away before it has a chance to harden.

If a tile sinks below the plane of the surrounding tiles, pry it out and butter the back with a putty knife; then reset it. While installing each course, be sure to check the work with the spirit level to be sure that the tiles are level. Correct deviations as soon as possible because any error in the row will multiply as successive rows are added. After a section of tiles has been installed, place the beating block over them and tap it with a rubber mallet to ensure that the tiles are firmly seated in the adhesive.

Be sure to keep a can of solvent nearby to clean off the surface of the tiles or wipe up adhesive spills as you work. Remember that most solvents are flammable, so take all necessary safety precautions when working with them.

After all the tiles are in place, the accessories can be mounted. It is best to hold off until the field tiles have adequate time to set so that installation of the accessory doesn't disturb adjacent tiles. Make sure that the surface where the accessory will fit is clean and dry and free of tile adhesive. Butter the back of the accessory with adhesive and then press it in place.

Most accessories are heavier than ordinary tiles, so it may be necessary to use a heavy-duty adhesive such as epoxy to secure them in place. After pressing the piece in place, use masking tape as a temporary support to hold it until the adhesive has had time to set.

Before applying the grout, allow at least 24 hours to give the adhesive time to cure. Clean the tile surface to make sure that all adhesive and debris is removed from the tiles. If the tiles are unglazed, apply a sealer before grouting. Again, allow 24 hours for the sealer to fully dry before proceeding.

Mix the grout according to the package directions and apply it with a grout float. Push the grout across the face of the tiles with the float held at a 30-degree angle. Make sure the grout is pressed into the gaps surrounding each tile, and then cut away excess grout with the float. This will remove most of the excess, but there will still be a film of grout across the surface of the field. If it is not removed, the grout will harden and leave a permanent haze on the tiles.

Use a grout sponge to wipe the surface clean. Keep in mind that this surface residue will begin to harden in a matter of minutes, while the grout packed in the joints will need hours to cure. Use a light touch when wiping the surface or else you will wear away the grout in the joints. The round corners of the grout sponge can also be used to shape and smooth the grout joints as the residue is being removed.

Allow time for the grout to thoroughly harden—this may take at least two weeks. Then clean the tile surface again. Apply a grout sealer with a foam roller or sponge and wipe away any excess with a clean rag.

8–15. *At first glance, the tiles around the opening to this fireplace might look like ordinary tiles with an off-white hue. Closer inspection, however, reveals that the tiles have a subtle relief that suggests the texture of the surrounding rocks around the fireplace without detracting from the rustic effect of the stones.* **(Photo courtesy of Lis King Tile Company)**

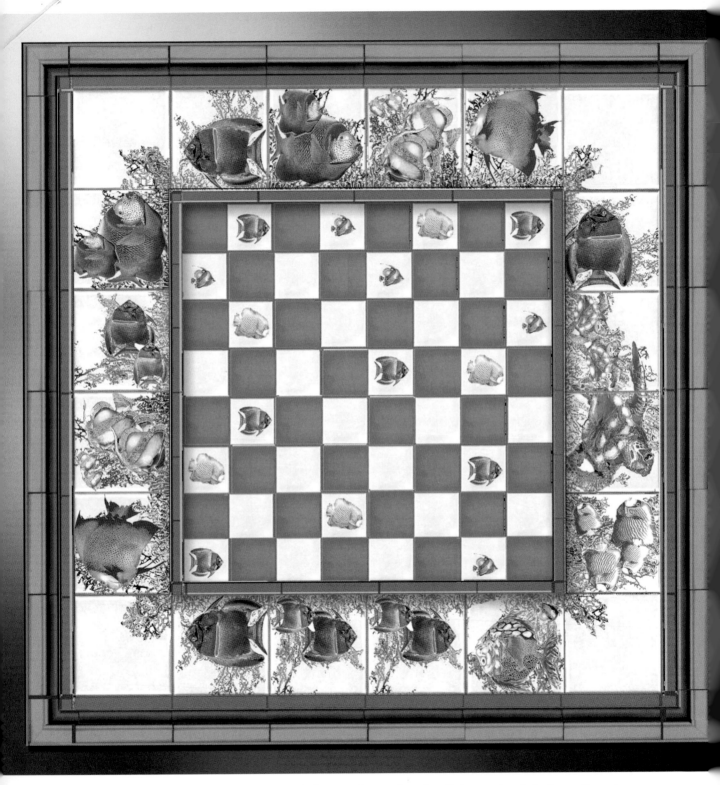

9–1. *Tiles less than two inches long are called mosaic tiles. For large installations, such as in bathroom floors, they are available in sheet form. However, for smaller projects they can be used in many creative ways. Here mosaic tiles and picture tiles are combined to form a tabletop that is also a chessboard.* **(Photo courtesy of M.E. Tile Company)**

Setting Mosaic Tiles

SHEET-MOUNTED MOSAIC TILES

While most do-it-yourselfers choose large—four inches or larger—tiles for either a floor or wall installation, there may be times when a smaller tile has more appeal. Tiles that are less than two inches are called mosaic tiles. Trying to set small tiles individually would be an arduous and frustrating task because it would be enormously time-consuming to try to align all the small pieces and maintain an even and consistent gap between them.

Fortunately, these tiles come mounted in sheet form, and this makes mosaic tile installation easier, if not exactly a piece of cake. Traditionally, sheet mosaics were face-mounted, that is, the paper that held the tiles together was attached to the face of the tiles. After the tiles were set in place and the underlying adhesive had cured, the paper was moistened and peeled away.

There were a number of disadvantages to this system. First, since the paper was opaque it was often difficult to be sure that the tiles were aligning properly. Also, it was almost impossible to tell whether excess adhesive had worked its way up in the gaps between the tiles. Finally, removing the paper and the residue adhesive that held the paper to the face of the tiles was often a tedious and messy procedure.

In an attempt to address and solve these problems, manufacturers soon came up with sheet tiles that had a gauze mounting material on the back. Another system for holding mosaics in sheet form is the dot mounting system. Here, the tiles are held together with small rubber or plastic circles, called dots, that bridge the gap between individual tiles. Since both systems use a holding medium positioned on the rear, not the face, of the tiles, they are called "back-mounted" tiles.

Back-mounted tiles are a definite improvement over face-mounted tiles, because the tile setter can see all the tiles as they are being pressed into place and he can make adjustments in alignment where necessary; and there is no paper to be peeled away afterward.

Still, there are problems with back-mounted tiles. The holding medium on the back of the tile does obscure some of the tile surface. This reduces the holding power of the adhesive.

In addition, dot-mounted tiles offer a unique problem because with some sheets the dots have an oily residue that can interfere with the bonding capacity of the adhesive. The best way to deal with the residue on the surface of the holding dots is by carefully examining the tile sheets before buying them. Take some paper towels with you when going to the tile shop. Wipe the surface of the dots with the towel to see if it picks up any oil. If so, ask the dealer for another lot and try again. If you do buy dot-mounted sheets and if there is an oily residue, remove it before attempting to install the tiles. Wash the back of the sheets with a solution of mild detergent and warm water. Rinse and then dry the tiles thoroughly. Do not attempt to mount tiles if the backs are wet.

Dealing with the problem of the backing material obscuring the tile backs is a little more difficult. The best solution is to apply the adhesive in a slightly thicker layer than normal and then use a beating block to pound the tiles into the setting bed. This technique forces the adhesive around the backing material and creates a strong bond with the tiles. But how can you determine that there is enough adhesive over the substrate? A quick test can be made after the first mosaic sheet has been set in place.

Before spreading any adhesive, check the setting bed carefully. It should be firm, hard, and entirely flat. While this is desirable with any tile installation, it is absolutely essential for a mosaic job because there are so many more grout lines that must be straight. Any imperfections in the setting bed will be magnified when the mosaic pattern is in place.

Mix and spread the adhesive according to package directions, and using the notched trowel recommended by the manufacturer. Start by spreading the adhesive on a small area of the bed. Press the mosaic sheet onto the fresh adhesive, and then place the beating block on the surface. Use a mallet to pound the block and force the sheet down into the adhesive.

Next, pull the sheet away, turn it over, and examine the back for coverage. The backs of all the tiles should be fully coated with adhesive. If not, try reworking the adhesive with a larger-notched trowel. (This may require a trowel with notches $1/4$ inch wide and $3/8$ inch deep.) Then use a flat trowel to spread a thin layer of adhesive directly on the back of the sheet. Remount the tiles and then continue with the installation.

This approach is effective, but it can create another problem. Frequently the beating block forces the adhesive up through the tile joints. This requires more cleanup time. It can also fill the gaps with adhesive so there is little room for the grout. Trying to fill the empty joints with grout may produce an installation that has a gap pattern with two noticeably different colors.

Some installers anticipate this problem by using an adhesive of the same color as the grout, for example, white adhesive with white grout or gray adhesive with gray grout. This is acceptable from a distance, but often close inspection will reveal a discernible difference in color between the two compounds.

Another possible solution is to use an epoxy thinset for both the adhesive and the grout. There are two kinds of epoxy adhesive. One uses sand and portland cement as the base powder. The other, commonly called 100 percent solids, uses a base of silica sand and dye. The latter epoxy is the best to use as adhesive and grout.

With epoxy, there is no need to clean the adhesive from the joints because the same compound will later be used to fill them. However, it is important to remove any overfill that may spread onto the surface of the tiles. If it is not removed, the residue will harden and bond to the tiles.

So, while working pause frequently to remove excess adhesive or grout whenever it collects on the tiles. The best method for cleaning is to use a plastic abrasive pad and a little water. Use only enough water to dis-

solve the residue—be careful that excess water doesn't seep into the joints and weaken the bond holding the tiles.

CREATING ORIGINAL MOSAICS FOR WALLS OR FLOORS

Mosaic tiles may be laid on walls or floors in patterns, pictures, or abstract compositions. While the results, if properly executed, will be pleasing and even dramatic, the technique is time-consuming. An expansive mosaic pattern may take weeks to plan and install. This usually necessitates isolating the wall or floor where the installation is located. Naturally this can be an inconvenience for the household until the composition is completed.

There is another way, however, that makes it possible to design and execute a mosaic weeks or months ahead of time and have it ready and waiting until the installation commences. It is called the "indirect method." This is opposed to the "direct method," where the tesserae are pressed directly into the thinset, one tile at a time, creating the total composition as you go along. The indirect method makes it possible to work in an area away from the actual tile installation and create the mosaic. It can then be secured to backing paper and moved to the installation when you are ready.

First, choose the work area where you can compose and execute the mosaic without being disturbed. Since the project may take several days (depending upon its complexity and your working skills), pick an area with little traffic. A large table (the size will depend upon the dimensions of the design) will be needed to set up the mosaic.

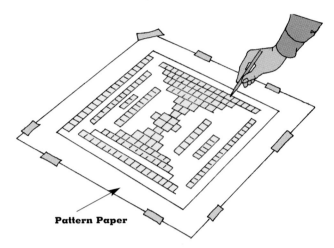

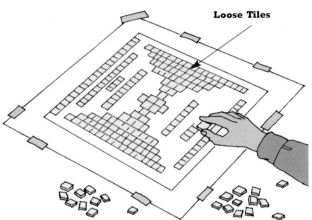

Pattern Paper

Loose Tiles

9-2. *The indirect method of mosaic installation allows you to design and execute a mosaic weeks or months ahead of time and have it ready and waiting until the installation commences. Start by drawing the design on a large sheet of pattern paper. Use colored pencils or markers to color the design.*

9-3. *When the design is complete, start laying tiles in place. Do not use glue or adhesive to hold the pieces in place; this is a dry run to check your composition. While placing the tiles, be sure to leave a gap between each one for the grout.*

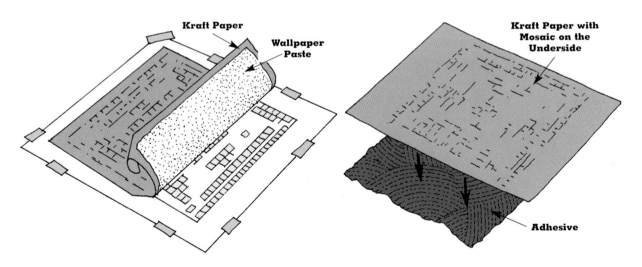

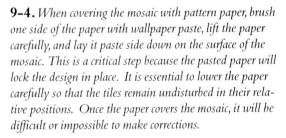

Kraft Paper

Wallpaper Paste

Kraft Paper with Mosaic on the Underside

Adhesive

9-4. *When covering the mosaic with pattern paper, brush one side of the paper with wallpaper paste, lift the paper carefully, and lay it paste side down on the surface of the mosaic. This is a critical step because the pasted paper will lock the design in place. It is essential to lower the paper carefully so that the tiles remain undisturbed in their relative positions. Once the paper covers the mosaic, it will be difficult or impossible to make corrections.*

9-5. *A face-mounted sheet mosaic that can be moved to an installation at the proper time. Do not move or disturb the mosaic until the paste has dried.*

Place a sheet of pattern paper, large enough to render the design, on the table (**9–2**). Secure it to the tabletop by tacking the corners down with masking tape. Next, draw a rectangle (or circle if the plan is round) large enough to contain the entire composition. Use colored pencils to draw and color the design within the rectangle.

When you are satisfied with the design, start laying the tiles in place. Do not use glue or adhesive to hold them in place; this is a dry run. With a normal tile installation, you are restricted to laying the tiles in a geometric pattern, cutting the tiles only to fit near a wall or around an obstacle. With mosaics, the tesserae can be cut and shaped to create lines and color patterns where this is needed. Use the tile nippers for cutting the tiles. When you place the tiles, be sure to leave a gap between each one for the grout (**9–3**).

With ordinary rectangular tiles, the grout gap should be consistent throughout the field, but this may not be possible with a mosaic because the tesserae may vary in size and shape. Still, it is a good practice to keep the grout gaps as uniform as possible.

When all the tiles are in position and you are satisfied with the composition, cut a piece of pattern paper large enough to cover the entire mosaic. Brush one side of the paper with wallpaper paste; then lift the paper carefully and lay it paste side down on the surface of the mosaic (**9–4**).

This is a critical step because the pasted paper will lock the design in place. It is essential to lower the paper slowly so that the tiles remain undisturbed in their relative position to the whole composition. Once the paper covers the mosaic it is almost impossible to make corrections, so work carefully and methodically.

Use a wallpaper smoothing brush or a rolling pin to press the paper onto the surface of the tiles. Should the paper wrinkle, do not

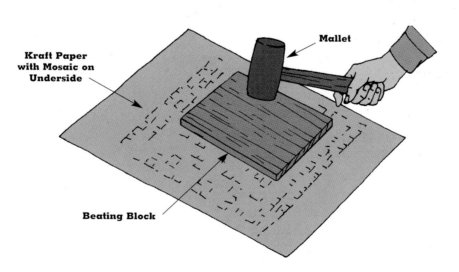

Kraft Paper with Mosaic on Underside

Mallet

Beating Block

9-6. *After the mosaics tiles have been pressed into the adhesive, use a beating block and mallet to make sure they are firmly seated. In addition to pressing the tiles into the underlying adhesive, the beating block will also help to ensure that the mosaic forms a level surface.*

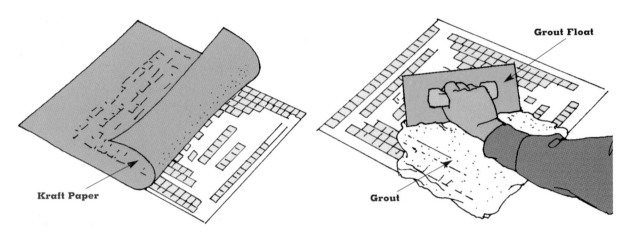

Kraft Paper

Grout Float

Grout

9-7. *Allow time for the adhesive to cure; then use a damp, but not dripping sponge to moisten the pattern paper. This will dissolve the wallpaper paste and allow you to pull the paper away from the mosaic without pulling up the tiles.*

9-8. *Grout all joints. Use a grout float, held at a 30-degree angle, to push the grout across the mosaic and into the gaps between the tiles. Remove excess grout with the float. Use a damp sponge or cloth to remove any remaining grout residue or haze.*

9-9. *Small tiles called tesserae are combined here with sculptural tiles to create an unusual countertop for a lavatory. While this artistic effect is highly imaginative and visually stimulating, it should not be used in high-traffic areas because it may be difficult to maintain.* **(Photo courtesy of M.E. Tile Company)**

attempt to lift the paper to smooth it out; instead use the brush or your hand to flatten the wrinkles.

Do not move or disturb the mosaic until the paste has dried. In effect, you have created a face-mounted sheet mosaic that can be moved to an installation when you are ready for it **(9–5)**. If the piece is particularly large, there may be difficulty moving it without the weight of the tiles tearing the paper.

There are two ways to handle this problem. A large piece of plywood or particleboard can be placed under the mosaic and taped in place. With the board as a support, you can carry the sheet to the installation site and carefully slide it (after releasing the hold-down tape) off the board onto the thinset bed of adhesive.

Another approach is to cut through the paper with a utility knife, thus dividing the mosaic into manageable sections. Carry the individual sections to the installation site and reassemble the mosaic there.

After the mosaic tiles have been pressed into the adhesive at the site, use a beating block and mallet to make sure they are firmly seated **(9–6)**. Allow time for the thinset to cure; then use a damp, but not dripping, sponge to moisten the pattern paper. When the wallpaper paste is wet and partially dissolved, gently peel away the paper, leaving the mosaic in the installation **(9–7)**. Grout and seal the joints as with an ordinary tile installation **(9–8)**.

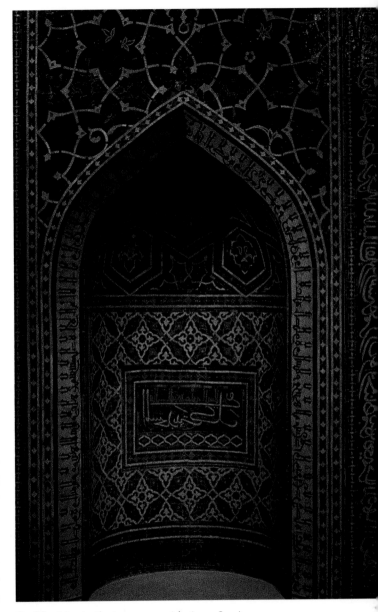

9–10. *Mosaic tiles in a prayer niche in an Iranian mosque.* **(Metropolitan Museum of Art)**

10–1. *Tiles used for outdoor installations should be selected with care because they must stand up to the freeze/thaw cycle and also to the intense heat of the sun. Also, all adhesives, grouts, sealants, and caulk should be formulated for outdoor use. Even though these materials may be designed for freezing environments, it is always best to work outdoors when the conditions are close to room temperature.* **(Photo courtesy of Crossville Porcelain Stone/USA)**

Outdoor Installations

Ceramic tile can provide a durable and elegant surfacing material for patios, outdoor walkways, or entranceways. However, it is more expensive than simple concrete, and for this reason it is important to plan the installation carefully to avoid costly mistakes.

First, it is important to choose the proper tiles. This will be determined by the climate conditions in your area. Vitreous or impervious tiles are the best choice for almost all locations because they do not absorb water and are therefore resistant to freeze/thaw cycles **(10–2)**. They should be used in all installations that will be subjected to rain and cold winter conditions. In warm, dry areas like the American Southwest you can get by

with nonvitreous pavers provided the weather remains relatively dry without extreme drops in the temperature. However, they should be sealed with an appropriate sealer to prevent moisture penetration. In those areas with extremely cold climates, it is best to avoid installing tiles on outdoor surfaces because they will deteriorate quickly in extreme freeze/thaw conditions.

Next, consider the concrete surface that will be tiled. It must be flat, and sloped to allow proper drainage. To check for drainage, look at the slab after a rainstorm. Numerous or large puddles on the surface indicate depressions and poor drainage. Correcting this problem will require resurfacing, or

10-2. *Vitreous or impervious tiles are the best choice for almost all locations because they do not absorb water and are therefore resistant to freeze/thaw cycles. They should be used in all installations that will be subjected to rain and cold winter conditions. The corner tiles on these steps are mitered to blend the convergent rows in a pleasing manner. It is a simple treatment, but it requires the ability to make accurate cuts.*

"floating," the slab with a thick bed of mortar. This is much like pouring a new slab of concrete, but requires technical skill to make sure the final surface is flat and sloped properly. The slope should drop 1/8 inch for every foot or 1 inch for every 8 feet.

Defects such as large cracks or buckling indicate unstable soil or a weak slab. These must be corrected before the tiles can be installed. Unfortunately, these are major problems that usually require pouring a new slab.

If the slab is stable and properly sloped, you can begin the installation by preparing the surface. It is important to remove any grease, dirt, or other contaminants that could adversely affect the adhesive that bonds the tiles. Scrub the concrete thoroughly with a commercial concrete cleaner (wear rubber gloves and eye protection because these cleaners can be harsh and irritating) and a stiff-bristled brush. After scrubbing, rinse the area thoroughly with water.

After rinsing, inspect the surface again to see if the rinse water beads up on the concrete surface. Beading usually indicates that an admixture was used in the concrete mix. Admixtures are materials other than portland cement, aggregates, or water that are added to concrete to modify its properties. In some cases, stearates or oils are added to make the final slab more waterproof.

This type of admixture can prevent the tile adhesive from bonding properly with the concrete slab, and, unfortunately, it cannot be removed by scrubbing. Nor is it a good idea to use a chemical remover, because the chemical remover may also have an adverse effect on the tile adhesive. You will need to remove the admixture by sandblasting or by waterblasting.

Next, inspect the surface for cracks and irregularities such as large pits or lumps. Patch and fill all cracks and pits with concrete patching material. Chisel away any lumps with a cold chisel and small sledgehammer **(10–3)**; then fill any resulting cavities with patching material **(10–4)**. Check also to see if the concrete has a polished or slick surface. This type of finish is undesirable because it cannot provide the necessary "tooth" for the tile adhesive. Here it is best to roughen the concrete surface with a power sander before the installation. After making all repairs, wash the surface again to remove any loose debris or dust.

At this point, you are ready to begin the installation. Measure the surface of the slab to determine the best size tiles to use. Ideally the slab dimensions should be multiples of full tiles. If not, you will have to cut some tiles or choose smaller tiles to fit around the field tiles. Planning to lay down tiles on an outdoor concrete slab is much the same as any floor installation, with one important nuance: concrete slabs have expansion joints. These do not prevent cracking, but they allow the cracks to develop along preplanned lines rather than in random patterns across the entire surface. If

10-3. *Before tiling an existing concrete surface, scrub and rinse the concrete thoroughly. Then inspect the surface for cracks and irregularities such as large pits or lumps. Chisel away any lumps with a cold chisel and small sledgehammer. Cracks, holes, and other damaged areas should be chiseled out to remove loose chips of concrete. At the same time, undercut the crack or hole to provide a key for the concrete patch.*

10-4. *After making all repairs, wash the surface again to remove any loose debris or dust. Brush the interior of the hole with water or a bonding agent. Mix the concrete filler according to the package directions. Using a trowel, pack the filler into the hole and smooth it.*

possible, plan to place the tiles so the grout joints are directly above these joints. This will ensure that the expansion and contraction of the concrete is transmitted to grout gaps and does not affect the tiles.

Ordinarily with a typical floor installation, it is only necessary to apply a single layer of adhesive and then press the tiles into it. With an outdoor slab, it is a good idea to trowel a thin bond coat over the entire surface with a smooth trowel and let it dry. Ideally, the adhesive should be spread when the ambient temperature is between 60 and 70 degrees F. Be sure to use latex additives with the adhesive and grout.

As with any tile installation, it is important to establish working lines that mark the center of the surface. After applying the bond coat of adhesive, snap chalk lines along the midpoints of the width and length of the slab. These lines should intersect to mark the center point of the slab. Start at the center point and spread the adhesive with a notched trowel. Remember that as time passes the adhesive will tend to "set up" or "skin over" (this is called the "working time"), after which it will not bond well with the tiles. Do not spread more adhesive than can be covered within the working time.

Start placing the tiles in the adhesive. Use a beating block to ensure that the tiles are firmly embedded and the tile surface is flat. Periodically pause to check the installation with a straightedge to be sure that the installation is level and true. After the entire field is in place, check to make sure that there is no adhesive ebbing through the grout gaps. If there is, remove it before it hardens. Allow sufficient time for the adhesive to cure; then apply an appropriate grout as recommended by the tile manufacturer. It is best to use caulk, not grout, in gaps that lie over the expansion joint. When the grout has hardened, apply a grout sealer.

POURING A NEW SLAB

If you do not have a concrete slab in place, one can be poured. Pouring a new slab does not require any sophisticated construction skills, but still it is not easy. It involves careful planning, excavation, construction of the proper forms, and base preparation before the concrete is poured. All this requires hard work, and, depending upon the size of the slab, at least two people to shovel and rake the concrete evenly over the entire surface.

Planning generally begins by making a scale drawing of the slab. To ensure minimum cutting, the dimensions should be multiplies of full tiles. Outdoor installations require wider grout joints, about $5/8$ inch depending upon the size of the tile, than interior plans. A good working drawing should also have all the expansion joints marked in position. With a scale drawing in hand, you should next check with the local authorities to obtain the necessary building permits and to ensure that your plans meet all specifications and codes.

The next step is to stake out the area on the actual site; then excavation can begin. Factors such as ground slope, soil condition, and climate conditions will determine the depth that is needed to excavate. You will have to excavate deep enough to accommodate the slab and also a gravel and sand bed. This will promote drainage and provide a stable base for the concrete slab. In areas with moderate rainfall, a four-inch gravel bed, under a two-inch

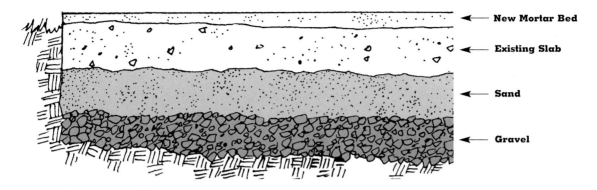

New Mortar Bed

Existing Slab

Sand

Gravel

10–5. *Before you can pour a slab, you will have to excavate deep enough to accommodate the slap and also a gravel and sand bed. This will promote drainage and provide a stable base for the concrete slab. In areas with moderate rainfall, a four-inch gravel bed under a two-inch bed of sand should provide a proper base for a slab. If the slab is already in place but has a damaged surface, or if the surface does not have the proper slope, you can resurface, or "float," the slab with a thick bed of mortar. The slope should drop $1/8$ inch for every foot or 1 inch for every 8 feet.*

bed of sand, should provide a proper base for a slab **(10–5)**. Soil with a higher moisture content will require deeper layers of gravel and sand, and possibly a layer of stone under these. In areas subject to frost heavals, it may also be necessary to plant a perimeter of concrete footing to support the slab.

For small slabs, you may be able to excavate with basic hand tools. For larger areas, power tools can be rented for the job. After removing the soil to the necessary depth, tamp down all loose soil. Next, build the necessary forms to contain the poured concrete. These are best built with standard construction lumber, either 2 X 4s or 2 X 6s. Make sure that they are staked and properly leveled.

When the forms are in place, fill in the gravel and sand beds to the proper depth. Compact the sand layer with a tamping tool and make sure that it is perfectly level and flat. Unless the slab is a small one, it should be reinforced with wire mesh or rebar (wire mesh is the easiest to install). Place the wire mesh over the sand bed and raise it with rocks

or brick fragments so it is about two inches above the sand surface. This will ensure that it is embedded in the center of the concrete slab **(10–6)**.

At this point, you are ready for the actual

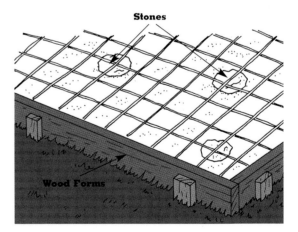

Stones

Wood Forms

10–6. *When the forms are in place, fill in the gravel and sand beds to the proper depth. Compact the sand layer with a tamping tool and make sure that it is perfectly level and flat. Unless the slab is a small one, it should be reinforced with wire mesh or rebar (wire mesh is the easiest to install). Place the wire mesh over the sand bed, and raise it with rocks or brick fragments so it is about two inches above the sand surface. This will ensure that it is embedded in the center of the concrete slab..*

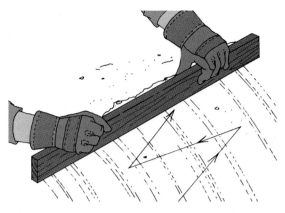

10–7. *Use a wide, wooden board as a screed to level the surface. Place the board on edge and work across the patch with a zigzag motion. Repeat until all the high spots are removed and the depressions are filled.*

concrete pour. For large jobs, it is best to call for wet mix. This is delivered by truck and is sold in cubic yards. Consult with the dealer to determine how many yards are required. If possible, provide access so the truck can unload directly into the forms. As you pour, rake and push the concrete over the entire surface, being sure to push it into all voids. When the concrete is in place, tamp it to remove all trapped air bubbles.

Level the surface by pulling a screed (essentially a four-foot length of 2 X 4) across the slab **(10–7)**. This will knock down any bumps and fill in possible depressions. Use a darby (a long wooden trowel, available at tool rental shops) to smooth the surface. Then use an edging tool to form rounded edges around the perimeter of the slab. Next, use a straightedge and jointed trowel to place the control joints.

After all this, wait about an hour for the concrete to "firm up"; then brush the surface with a stiff-bristled push broom. This will texture the surface and create the necessary "tooth" for the tile adhesive **(10–8)**.

The final step is to allow the necessary time for the concrete to cure properly. Concrete cures best if it does not dry out too quickly. This hydration retention allows the concrete to harden into a durable and water-resistant material. To ensure maximum hydration retention during the curing process, cover the entire slab with polyethylene sheeting for about a week. The sheeting will keep moisture within the slab as it cures. After it cures, it can be tiled.

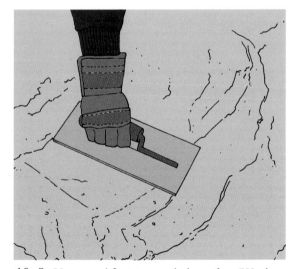

10–8. *Use a wood float to smooth the surface. (Wood floats will create a rough texture that provides the necessary "tooth" for the tile adhesive.) Hold the float flat on the concrete and move it back and forth across the patch in wide arcs.*

10–9. *This installation is in a sheltered area under a porch roof, but it is still considered an outdoor installation. The tiles will not be exposed to the harsh sunlight but will still have to withstand the freeze/thaw cycle. They are laid in a herringbone pattern. Laying down tiles in this pattern requires careful planning and involves a considerable amount of cutting. It is best to rent a wet saw for this type of installation.* **(Photo courtesy of Lis King Tile Company)**

Troubleshooting Problems

A good tile surface should last for many years without problems. Eventually though, even the best installations can develop problems: cracks may develop in the grout, the tiles may crack or work loose from the underlying bed, and water stains may appear around the tiles.

Sometimes the causes for these maladies may be relatively minor and the damage can be easily corrected. In other cases what may seem like a small problem, a number of

11–1 (opposite page). *All installations, including this well-executed kitchen installation, will eventually develop problems. Knowing how to examine each problem carefully and determine the cause and extent of the damage is important.*

cracked tiles, for example, can actually be a major headache if the underlying structure is flawed. It is important then to examine each problem carefully to determine the cause and the true extent of the damage.

GROUT PROBLEMS

When the grout between the tiles begins to crack or deteriorate, it may mean that the expansion joints around the surface are inadequate or the grout was improperly mixed or applied. It is important to inspect the surface and evaluate the problem before attempting any corrective action.

If the grout cracks are around the perimeter of the tile surfaces, that is, near adjacent walls, floors, or fixtures (for example, the bathtub), then the cracks are probably the result of expansion or contraction between the two surfaces. Since the grout is a hard and relatively rigid material, it cannot adjust to the shifts in large areas. The best solution to the problem is to remove the grout and substitute a flexible caulk.

If the expansion joints are in good shape, then the cracks are probably caused by deterioration in the grout itself. This can happen if the grout was mixed with too much liquid or absorbed too much water during cleanup. A grout mixture with too much liquid would lose much of its adhesive strength and crack and deteriorate over time.

The problem cannot be corrected simply by applying new grout over the old, because

11-2. *Use a grout saw to remove damaged grout. Work carefully to avoid damaging the nearby tiles. Clear the grout down to the substrate, but do not damage the substrate. This is particularly important if there is a waterproof membrane beneath the tiles. After sawing away the grout, use a damp, stiff-bristled brush to clean out the gaps between the tiles.*

grout is a relatively inflexible material and is not strong or durable in thin layers. Eventually the added grout will flake off and expose the deteriorated material below. To correct the problem, it is necessary to first remove the old grout from the gaps between the tiles.

A utility knife or a piece of hacksaw blade can be used to remove old grout, but these tools are makeshift at best. For a quality job, it is best to invest in either a grout saw or a hook-shaped carbide-scoring tool. (These are available at home centers and ceramic tile stores.) Use these tools to saw or scrape away all traces of the crumbling grout **(11–2)**. Clean the gaps down to the substrate, but be careful not to damage the substrate below. Use a vacuum cleaner to suck out all the dust and debris from the gaps; then clean the surface of the tiles.

Hand tools are good for removing crumbling grout from a few joints, but for large installations this method may prove tedious. There is a power tool that makes this job much easier. It is a small hand grinder that can be fitted with a carbide-tipped rotary file **(11–3)**. The file is specially designed to remove grout. A number of manufacturers offer hand grinders that accept the file bit.

As convenient as this tool is, it takes a steady hand to guide it along the grout lines. If you get careless and slip, the carbide bit will cut into the surrounding tiles. One company, Sears, offers a grout removal attachment that will fit on its hand grinder. It has a collar with special guides that help to move the file bit along the grout joints without damaging the nearby tiles.

Many ceramic-tile stores sell products

11-3. *Removing crumbling or discolored grout can be a tedious and difficult job. There are hand tools such as a grout saw that are designed for this task, but for large jobs it is best to use a power tool. This hand grinder is fitted with a rotary grout saw. A special collar mounted around the saw blade guides the saw so the blade does not cut into surrounding tiles.* **(Photo courtesy of Sears, Roebuck and Company)**

11-4. *Probably the most difficult part of installing new grout is finding a product that matches the color of the existing grout (this is not a problem if the grout is white). If possible, take a sample of the old grout to a tile store and use it to compare the color and texture of products so a good match can be found. Mix the grout according to package directions; then apply it to the tile surface with a grout float.*

that are specifically made to clean grout residue (often called "grout haze"), or a good substitute can be made by mixing a cup of vinegar in a gallon of clean water. This mildly acidic solution is effective in removing grout residue and also the grease and soap scum that often collect on tile surfaces. Allow the area to dry completely before applying the grout.

Probably the most difficult part of installing new grout is finding a product that matches the color of the existing grout. If possible, take a piece of the old grout with you when visiting the tile store. Often the dealer will have grout samples so you can compare the color and texture of the various products to find a good match. If you cannot

11-5. *Remove excess grout with the float; then wipe away any remaining residue or haze with a grout sponge. Unlike an ordinary sponge, the grout sponge has rounded corners that can be used to dress the gaps without pulling out the grout.*

match the exact color, then either pick the nearest complement or remove all of the old grout and replace it with new material **(11–4)**.

Mix the grout according to the package directions, fill all the joints carefully, and then clean away all the residue **(11–5)**.

TILE PROBLEMS

Tiles can sometimes work loose from the substrate **(11–6)**. If this happens, it usually indicates a problem with the adhesive bond. Sometimes the adhesive may have dried slightly (called "skinning over") before the tiles were positioned, or perhaps something on the back of the tiles or on the substrate prevented a good bond. In any case, it is important to examine the back of the tile and the surface of the exposed substrate to diagnose the extent of the problem.

Inspect both to see how much adhesive still adheres to either surface. If only one tile has worked loose and the adhesive is largely on the substrate, then it's likely that the back of the tile was dirty and the adhesive could not adhere properly. Here it is only necessary to scrape the old adhesive off the substrate, apply a new coating, and install a new tile.

If a number of tiles have popped loose, then the adhesive probably skinned over before the tiles were set. Here the problem is more serious, and it's likely that more tiles will work loose soon. The sure solution involves removing all the tiles and underlying adhesive, and then setting the tiles. Obviously, this is a major undertaking and it may not be worth the time, money, and effort if the majority of tiles are firmly bonded to the substrate.

The vexing problem is: how to tell if those tiles are firmly in place or ready to pop up unexpectedly? Unfortunately, there are no certain methods to determine the extent of the problem. Some tile setters tap each tile with a metal tool, such as a small file or wrench; if the tap produces a ringing sound, then the tile is probably anchored securely **(11–7)**. If the sound is more like a dull "thud," then the tile is not secure. Other setters try to gently pull up on the edges of a few tiles with their finger (they do not use a tool for this); tiles that come up are obviously loose and need resetting. Finally, some people simply adopt a "wait-and-see" attitude, and do nothing until the problem becomes acute.

Although tiles are usually sturdy and durable, they can still crack. One or two cracked tiles are usually not a cause for concern. Tiles will sometimes crack if there is a defect in the clay, that is, if the ingredients in the bisque were not uniformly distributed before the tile firing. This rarely happens when tiles are mass-produced by a major manufacturer, because these firms have rigid quality control. But the handmade tiles produced by small, independent manufacturers are less uniform, and are therefore more likely to crack or break.

Tiles can also crack or break if something is dropped on them. Obviously this is not the result of a defect in the tile. In either case, the only solution is to replace the tile. First, of course, you have to remove the old, damaged tile. The best way to do this is by striking it with a hammer and cold chisel to break it up, and then remove the pieces. Before striking the tile, first open up the joints around the perimeter of the tile by removing all the grout. This will isolate the tile and keep the impact of the hammer and chisel from cracking the neighboring tiles.

When the damaged tile is removed, use a floor scraper to remove all traces of the old adhesive. If this adhesive is not removed, it will be impossible to seat the new tile so it is level with the surrounding tiles. Make sure that all traces of the old adhesive and grout are removed; then vacuum the area to pick up any remaining dust or debris.

Apply fresh adhesive by buttering the back of the new tile; then press the tile in place. Wipe away any adhesive that oozes up around the joints. Wait at least 24 hours for the adhesive to dry, and then grout the joints. On vertical surfaces, it may be necessary to tape the tile in place until the adhesive cures.

If a crack runs through an entire row of tiles, it indicates a problem with the substrate or supporting structure. If the tiles were installed over an expansion joint between two dissimilar materials, they could crack if the substrate expands or contracts. Sometimes the

11-6. *The damage illustrated here shows a few loose tiles in a floor installation of mosaic tiles. Careful inspection reveals a large dent or depression around the damaged area. This indicates that the damage may be the result of a heavy weight that was dropped on the floor. The repair procedure requires removing the loose tiles and maybe some of the secure ones around the depression, and then leveling the substrate with adhesive. In this installation, the original adhesive was not thinset, but mortar. This will require mixing a small amount of mortar to secure the damaged tiles.*

11-7. *Sometimes it is possible to test the tiles to see if they are firmly in place by tapping them with a metal tool such as a rod or a wrench. If the tap produces a ringing sound, then the tile is probably anchored securely. If the sound is more like a dull "thud," then the tile is not secure.*

problem can be corrected by removing the tiles and underlying adhesive, and then installing a special isolation membrane over the problem area. It's best to consult with a dealer or professional tile setter to see if this can work in your case. Once the membrane is in place (read the manufacturer's specifications for installation procedures), the tiles can be reset.

A large crack may also appear if the substrate under the tiles is not rigid enough. Usually the subfloor under the tiles is too thin, so it flexes whenever weight is applied. The tiles, being less flexible, will snap rather than bend with the floor. The way to correct the problem is by bracing the floor so it will not flex or bend.

Sometimes this can be done easily if the underside of the floor is exposed. If, for example, it is a ground floor over an unfinished basement, it may be possible to add additional framing members between the joists. If the floor cannot be braced from below, the tiles should be removed so another layer of substrate can be added.

There is another way to correct the problem, although it is not as effective as strengthening the floor. After the damaged tiles are replaced, the joints on either side should be filled with flexible caulk. This will provide an expansion joint on either side of the tiles that may isolate them from the rest of the floor; but, of course, the caulk will not match the grout in all the other joints.

Water Stains

Water stains are obviously not caused by the tiles, but from leaks in the nearby plumbing. In some cases, a small hole in the roof or wall may allow rainwater to enter behind the tile surface and create the stains. This is not, strictly speaking, a tile problem. The solution involves finding and isolating the leak—this may entail refitting the plumbing or patching the roof—and then removing and replacing the tiles. If the substrate is damaged, it should also be replaced.

Lipping

Lipping is an alignment problem that occurs during installation. Sometimes, no matter how carefully you work to set the tiles, a few will have adjoining edges that either do not align or rise slightly above the surrounding plane. This is usually caused by a defect in the tiles and not in the setting technique. Often the tiles were warped or deformed during the manufacturing process; this occurs more with handmade tiles than mass-produced pieces.

Sometimes the misalignment can be "adjusted" by adding a little more adhesive, that is, buttering the back, under the tile, or by adjusting the grout joint. In most cases, however, the best solution is to grind the offending edge with a rough stone. Tiles that have severe distortions should be sent to a dealer that specializes in stone refinishing.

GLOSSARY

Abrasion Resistance The ability of a tile surface to withstand or resist wear by friction.

Acrylic Thinset Adhesive A sand-and-cement thinset adhesive that is mixed with an acrylic additive before use.

Aggregate Inert material that is added to a mixture such as grout to increase strength in wide joints.

Anchor A metal-securing device driven into wood, concrete, or masonry.

ANSI (American National Standards Institute) A nonprofit, nontechnical institution founded in 1918 for the purpose of increasing knowledge and promoting standards in industry. Formerly the American Standards Association (ASA) and the United States of America Standards Institute (USASI).

Apron Tiles Half-sized tiles used in narrow areas, such as the front edge of a countertop.

Azulejos Blue and white wall tiles manufactured in Portugal or Spain.

Backbuttering The technique of spreading adhesive on the back of a tile.

Backer Board (also known as "cementitious backer board.") A sheet product made up of cement with reinforcing layers of fiberglass mesh. Backer boards are available in thicknesses of $1/4$, $5/16$, $7/16$, $1/2$, and $5/8$ inch and in sheets 32 to 48 inches wide and 3 to 10 feet long. They are water-resistant, but should not be used in wet areas without a waterproof membrane.

Back-Mounted Tiles Tiles marketed in sheet form with the binding material on the back of the tiles.

Backsplash (sometimes called a "splashback") The short vertical wall that rises up at the rear of a countertop, sink, or stove or between the top of a base cabinet and the base of an upper unit.

Baseboard Wide molding attached to the wall where it joins the floor.

Base Coat A paint or plaster coat applied to a surface before the final coat.

Base Material (also called "backfill") Gravel, rubble, or other material used to fill over an excavation or to provide a stable base and drainage for footings and slabs.

Base Tiles Tiles with a finished top edge designed for setting along the floor line.

Batten Board A narrow strip of wood nailed or screwed temporarily in place. Its main purpose is to serve as a guide to align tiles as they are being installed.

Beating Block A block of wood used to seat tiles firmly. The block is placed over the newly installed tiles and tapped with a mallet.

Bicottura An early tile-making process where the tiles were fired to produce hard-bodied tiles, and then glazed and fired again. Bicottura was largely replaced by the monocottura process.

Bisque Refined clay that has been shaped into a tile or biscuit. An unfired bisque is called "green" bisque.

Bleeding The penetration of color from one layer of paint into another. Bleeding action occurs because of the solvent action of the last layer of paint applied or because the first layer was not allowed time to dry sufficiently. Often applying a primer over a layer of paint will seal the color in and prevent bleeding. In concrete applications, water that rises to the surface of newly poured concrete is called "bleeding."

BOCA (Building Officials Conference of America) A nonprofit organization that publishes the National Building Code.

Bond The ability of two surfaces to cling to one another. *See also* Chemical Bond and Mechanical Bond.

Bond Coat A layer of adhesive applied in a thin coat to the substrate.

Bond Strength The ability of an adhesive to hold a tile in place and resist separation.

Brads Small wire finishing nails, no longer than $1^1/_2$ inches, used to hold small pieces of wood in place without being visible.

Brick-Veneer Tiles Tiles made with surfacing designed to resemble brick and applied to a wall to create the impression of solid-brick construction. In some cases the tiles may actually be made of thin slices of real brick, or the tiles may be made from extruded mortar and textured to look like brick. This tile does not wear well and should not be used for floor applications.

Building Felt Asphalt-impregnated cloth or paper, sometimes erroneously called "tar paper."

Bullnose Tiles Tiles with one edge rounded over to a finish. They are used to finish a course, creating a margin (a distinct perimeter). They can also be used in combination with apron tiles to create a smooth turned corner.

Butt-Edged Tiles Tiles with flat, unfinished edges on all sides.

Button-Backed Tiles Tiles with small protuberances on the back. These raised dots help separate the tiles and promote airflow when the tiles are stacked in the kiln.

Carborundum Stone A coarse-grit stone made of silicon carbide. Used as an abrasive tool to smooth rough-cut edges of ceramic tile and backer board.

Casing The trim around windows and doors. *See also* Molding.

Caulk A flexible joint compound designed to fill gaps between the tiled surface and another material, for example the edge of a bathtub. Caulks may be latex-, acrylic-, rubber-, or silicone-based.

Caulking Gun A tool used to dispense caulk. There are two types. One accepts cartridges; the other, called a "full-barrel gun," has a chamber that accepts bulk caulking compound.

Cement-Bodied Tiles Tiles made of portland cement. A durable tile, less expensive than ceramic tile, it is often textured to look like stone or pavers.

Ceramic Fired clay material with or without a glaze.

Chalk Line A straight working line made by snapping a chalk-impregnated cord against a surface. The term "chalk line" may also refer to the chalk string used to snap the line. Although a chalk line may be improvised by drawing a length of string across a piece of colored chalk, professional models have the line in a case that is filled with chalk dust. As the line is withdrawn through an orifice in the case, it is automatically coated with chalk powder.

Chemical Bond The bond between two surfaces resulting from a chemical reaction.

Chlorinated Polyethylene (CPE) Membrane A plastic sheet made of CPE to be used as a waterproof membrane.

Cladding Wallboard or backer board applied to framing as a substrate.

Clay A mixture of kaolin, quartz in the form of sand, and small quantities of other minerals such as iron and feldspar.

Cleats Blocks or short boards mounted on a surface for the purpose of supporting braces or other members.

Cleft Stone Tile that is split, rather than sawn, from a large stone. Cleft stone tiles are uneven in thickness and vary in dimensions.

Closet Bolts (also called "hold-down bolts") The two bolts that project upward from the floor flange to hold a toilet bowl in place.

Cohesion The ability of a substance to bond or stick to itself.

Cold Chisel A chisel made from hexagonal sectional steel and used for cutting or chipping hard materials such as iron, steel, and masonry.

Common Nails Nails with large, round, flat heads that offer great holding power. They are used for general carpentry, but not finish work. Designated in penny sizes indicated by the letter "d", which indicates the length of the nail. The shortest is 2d, one inch. The longest, 60d, is six inches long.

Compression The force that presses the particles of a material closer together. A form of material stress.

Compression Strength The maximum ability of a material such as tile to withstand a heavy load without fracturing. Expressed as force per unit cross-sectional area, for example pounds per square inch (psi).

Contour Gauge (also called "profile gauge") A tool used to copy the contour or profile of a surface with a complicated shape. The tool consists of a holder with a row of tightly packed needles. When pressed against a surface, such as molding, the needles slide back to reproduce the shape of the molding.

Control Joint Grooves cut into a concrete surface to allow for the expansion and contraction of the material. The joints allow cracks to form in a planned manner rather than as random splits across the surface.

Countertop Tile Trim tiles with raised edges. They are shaped to fit over the outside edge of a countertop. The edge is designed to contain spills.

Course A complete horizontal row of tiles.

Cove Tiles Tiles with a curved profile. They are used in corners (for example, the corner where a floor and wall meet) to provide a smooth, rounded transition between right-angle surfaces.

Crazing A network of fine hairline cracks that often appear on old or stressed tiles. Intentional crazing during the manufacturing process for aesthetic effect should always be indicated by the manufacturer.

Cross Bracing (also called "bridge bracing") Short bracing between framing or structural members to add additional support. The pieces may be in the form of short solid lengths of construction lumber, lightweight boards, or metal.

CTI (Ceramic Tile Institute of America) A trade organization founded in 1954 for the purpose of upgrading standards and promoting excellence in installation methods. It offers consultation to builders and professionals on trade issues and legal matters and also offers a course of study called the Ceramic Tile Course. A list of certified tile installers is available on request.

Curing The period of time required for concrete, adhesive, or grout to reach its maximum holding strength.

Curing Membrane A thin film laid on a newly poured mortar bed. The membrane is designed to contain the moisture in the mortar and prevent premature curing of the bed. Also, a waterproof membrane that is laid down between a substrate and a mortar bed. The membrane isolates the substrate from the mortar and prevents it (the substrate) from absorbing moisture from the mortar and hampering the curing process. In most cases, the membrane is made of a plastic material, but for some concrete applications it can also be a liquid.

Damp Proofing Treatment of a surface by application of chemical sealers or a suitable film, such as polyethylene, to prevent the absorption of water, or water vapor. *See also* Waterproofing Membrane.

Deck The horizontal surface around a bathtub.

Delftware Blue and white glazed tiles, sometimes with polychrome decoration, originally made in Holland.

Dot-Mounted Tiles Tiles in sheet form held together with small plastic or rubber dots that bridge the gaps between the individual tiles.

Double-Headed Nail A nail with two heads used to nail a temporary brace or batten in place. The lower head secures the piece. The upper head allows a removal tool to grip the nail and remove it.

Down Angle Trim tiles with two dressed edges used for finishing outside corners.

Dressing A technique for smoothing and/or shaping a surface or joint.

Dry Mix Mortar or adhesive that comes prepackaged with all the ingredients except water.

Dry-Set Mortar A cement-based adhesive. It is called "dry-set" because it can be left to cure without the need to periodically dampen the surface.

Drywall (also called "wallboard," "gypsum board," or "Sheetrock," a trade name of The United States Gypsum Company) A generic term for an interior surfacing material made of gypsum plaster molded into sheets and faced on both sides with heavy paper. It is called "drywall" because it is mounted to the framing members in a dry state, in contrast to plaster, which must be mixed and applied wet. Drywall is available in thicknesses of $^1/_4$, $^3/_8$, $^1/_2$, and $^5/_8$ inch and in lengths from 6 to 16 feet with a standard width of 4 feet.

Drywall Nail A steel nail with either ringed grooves or a cement coating on its shank. It is available in lengths between $1^1/_4$ to $2^1/_8$ inches and in shank diameters of #12, 13, and 14 (American wire gauge).

Drywall Saw A short saw with coarse teeth used to cut drywall quickly.

Dust-Pressed Tiles Tiles formed by compressing dry clay dust and a small amount of water under heavy pressure.

Edger A tool for finishing the edges of a concrete surface.

Efflorescence The deposit of salts and minerals that shows up on a masonry surface as white crystals. The salts and minerals emerging through the walls are in solution. As the water evaporates, the crystals are left behind. Efflorescence indicates a water problem that should be corrected before attempting to install tiles on the surface.

Embossed-Back Tiles Tiles with manufacturer's identifying marks embossed on the back.

Encaustic A design in tile made by inlaying different-colored clays in the tile body.

Epoxy Thinset Adhesive A sand-and-cement thinset adhesive that is mixed with an epoxy resin additive before use.

Expansion Joint A control joint created by inserting a flexible material between fields of tile. The expansion joint absorbs the contraction and expansion of the fields and prevents damage to either.

Extruded Cement-Bodied Tiles Tiles composed of a mixture of portland cement and fine aggregate and made by the extrusion process and steam-cured. The tile may also be stained and sealed. The result is a dense-bodied tile with a tough surface (that may be textured in the extruding process) that is very durable and excellent for floor applications. It is not a good choice for wet or outdoor applications because it is not freeze/thaw stable.

Extruded Tiles Tiles formed by forcing green bisque through a fixed orifice, or die, to form a long continuous shape that is later cut to length.

Face-Mounted Tiles Tiles packaged in sheet form with a paper backing mounted on the face of the tile.

Field Tiles Tiles set in the main tract, or field, of an installation.

Finishing Nail A nail with a thin head that can be set below the wood's surface. As with common nails, finishing nails are sold by length designated in penny (d) size.

Firing The heat treatment of tiles. Firing temperatures range from as low as 900° F to a high of 2,500° F. Firing removes the moisture from the bisque and makes the tiles hard and dimensionally stable.

Float A tool used to smooth and finish a surface.

Floated Bed A bed of mortar that serves as a substrate or setting base for tile.

Form A temporary support structure or mold designed to hold and shape concrete as it cures.

Form Oil A lubricant, generally oil, applied to the inside of a form to allow it to release after the concrete hardens.

Framing The skeleton-like structure of a house or building that the sheathing, wallboard, subflooring, and ceilings are mounted on. Framing is done with construction-grade lumber, for example, 2 × 4s, or more recently with steel pieces having the same dimensions as construction-grade lumber.

Freeze/Thaw Cycle The ability of a material to expand and contract with changing temperature and humidity conditions without cracking.

Frost-Resistant Tiles Tiles that are dimensionally stable during a freeze/thaw cycle and are thus suitable for outdoor applications.

Furring Strips Narrow strips of wood attached to a surface, usually masonry, to even it out or to provide a base for nailing or bonding a new surfacing material.

Gauge The thickness of a tile.

Gauged Stone Stone tiles that have been cut and sometimes polished to uniform dimensions.

Ghosting Color change in grout joints caused by impurities in the grout mixture.

Glass Cutter A small, handheld tool with a cutting wheel at one end. It is used to score glass or ceramic tile.

Glaze A transparent glassy coating, either clear or colored, applied to a tile surface for aesthetic as well as protective purposes. Typical ceramic glazes consist of three ingredients. Silicates form the glass coating. Metallic oxides from lead or aluminum control the viscosity of the glaze during the firing and give the coating extra strength. A flux lowers the melting point of the silica. Other materials such as carbide particles may also be added to give the tiles a nonslip surface.

Green Bisque An unfired clay tile.

Grip Another term for bond strength.

Ground Edges Edges that have been cut and shaped to sharp 90-degree angles.

Grout A mixture of cementitious material and water with or without aggregates (sand). Grout is used as a binder and filler in the joints between the tiles. Most grout comes in powder form and must be mixed with water (latex or acrylic additive may be used instead of water to give added strength to the mixture) prior to application; a few, used mostly for patchwork, are ready-mixed. Ordinary grout, that is, grout without sand, is used in joints less than $1/16$ inch wide. Sand is added for grout used to fill wider joints to reduce shrinkage and prevent cracking.

Grout Sponge A sponge used for removing excess grout from a newly tiled wall. Grout sponges differ from ordinary sponges in that they have curved corners. This makes it easy to use the sponge to shape the grout joints.

Hang The ability of tiles to remain in position on a vertical surface as the adhesive sets.

Harsh Mixture Any mixture that lacks workability due to insufficient amounts of water or aggregate.

Hearth The fireproof surface positioned in front of a fireplace opening. The hearth may be level with the surrounding floor or raised above it.

Hot-Mopped Pan A shower pan (lining in the floor of a shower), no longer used today, made of alternating layers of building felt and hot asphalt.

ICBO (International Conference of Building Officials) A nonprofit organization that publishes the Uniform Building Code.

Impervious Tiles Dense-bodied tiles (denser than non-vitreous tiles) that have a water absorption of less than 0.5 percent. Compressive strength varies with different makes of impervious tile. Impervious tiles are fired at a high temperature for an extended time to make them waterproof and stable in a freeze/thaw cycle.

In-Corner Tiles Tiles that bend at a right angle. In-corner tiles are designed to turn a corner and join one tiled wall to another.

Inserts Smaller decorative tiles that are included with larger plain tiles to create patterns.

Inside Corner A joint formed when two flat surfaces meet at an angle less than 180 degrees.

Interior Wall A wall that faces inside a structure, as opposed to an exterior wall that faces outside the structure.

Isolation Joint A flexible material placed between two dissimilar materials (such as wood and tile). The joint acts as a buffer to absorb the expansion rates of the two materials.

Isolation Membrane (also called a "cleavage membrane") A thin, flexible sheet laid down on a setting bed to prevent unequal seasonal movement between layers.

Jack-on-Jack A common setting pattern for installing tiles. The courses of the tiles rise and align vertically. The tiles start in a corner (which must be perfectly square for the pattern to look even) and rise in rows. All grout gaps align vertically. The other common setting pattern is a running bond.

Joist A beam that supports a floor.

Kaolin The purest form of tile clay, made by repeated washing to remove all the impurities. Basically kaolin is a form of aluminum silicate.

Latex or Acrylic Thinset Adhesive A thinset tile adhesive containing sand and cement and mixed with liquid latex or acrylic prior to application.

Lath Thin wood slats or steel mesh used to support plaster walls.

Layout Lines Lines marked on a substrate and used to guide in proper installation and alignment of the tiles.

Layout Pole (also called a "story" or "jury stick"). A straight, narrow measuring stick marked in increments of the individual tile widths and the grout joints in between. The stick is used for making quick layouts and projecting the placement of a course of tiles in an installation.

Leather-Hardened Tiles Bisque that has air-dried to form rigid, less-pliable tiles. Leather-hardening tile is the final step before firing.

Level (also called a "spirit level" or "plumb rule") A tool used to determine whether a surface is perfectly horizontal or vertical, that is, "plumb and true." Levels consist of a wooden or metal case with straight, flat sides and one or more sight vials containing liquid and a bubble. When the surface is "true," the bubble will come to rest in the center of the vial. Levels come in lengths from 9 to 78 inches. There are also levels that use a laser beam instead of a liquid vial to determine if a surface is perfectly flat.

Leveling Mortar A mortar made of portland cement and selected additives and used in thin layers to level an uneven floor.

Lipping A condition that occurs on a flat surface when one or more tiles rise above the surrounding plane.

Lugs Projections on the sides of tiles designed to ensure even spacing.

Luster Iridescent glaze created by adding metallic particles from copper, silver, or gold to the glaze mix before firing.

Majolica A yellow-pink bisque with a nontransparent glaze. It is used primarily for indoor applications.

Mastic A term used to designate organic-based adhesives. *See also* Organic Mastic.

Medium-Bed Thinset Mortar A mortar used primary for floor applications where the floor surface may be irregular or in installations where the tiles vary in shape and/or thickness. This type of mortar is specially formulated to be laid down in thicker cross sections than regular thinset adhesives.

Membrane A thin, flexible sheet of material like building felt or polyethylene. Membranes are laid down to: prevent moisture from penetrating to the substrate (waterproofing membrane); control unequal seasonal expansion (isolation membrane); control curing of mortar beds (curing membrane); and dampen ambient noise (sound-control membrane).

Mesh Steel wire screening used to reinforce mortar. Also wire screening is used in the aggregate industry to shift sand and grade it into various-sized particles. The particle size is determined by the number of holes per inch in the mesh.

Mitered Joint Two pieces cut at a 45-degree angle. When they are joined together, they create a right, or 90-degree, angle.

Molding Boards milled in a variety of decorative profiles. Moldings are designed to add decorative accents to surfaces and to hide gaps between surfaces. Installed molding is called finish carpentry. Molding installed around doors and windows is called casing.

Monocottura A tile-making process in which tiles that are bisqued and glazed are fired in one operation. The monocottura process replaced the earlier bicottura process.

Monopressatura A tile-making process developed in Italy for the production of large (in sizes up to 24 inches x 24 inches) porcelain tiles. Basically the process consists of sandwiching a mixture of bisque and dry glaze ingredients in a compact layer and moving it through a kiln.

Mortar Material usually, but not always, made of cement paste and fine aggregate. There are various types of mortar. These include brick and block mortar, setting-bed mortar, thinset mortar, grout mortar, and leveling mortar.

Mosaic A picture or design composition made up of mosaic tiles.

Mosaic Tiles Glass or ceramic tiles less than two inches square. Mosaic tiles may come in preformed sheets on either paper or gauze backing or be sold individually. Mosaic tiles are very durable and may be used for floor as well as wall applications. Individual mosaic tiles are called "tessera" by mosaic artists.

Mud A common term used by tile setters to designate mortar or a mortar base.

Nail Set A tool used to drive nail heads below the surface of wood. The resulting holes are then filled with wood filler so the nail heads will be hidden.

Nonvitreous Tiles Tiles that absorb 7 percent of their weight in water. They are a cheaper tile because they are fired at a low temperature (requiring less time and energy). Nonvitreous tiles should not be used in wet areas or for outdoor applications.

NTCA (National Tile Contractors Association) A trade organization that works with the Tile Promotion Board. It has consultants to answer questions on tile installations and it will provide a list of NTCA member installers in any locale.

On Center (o.c.) A term used to designate the distance from the center of one framing member to the center of another. Means the same as center to center.

Open Time The length of time that an adhesive may remain exposed to the air before it dies out and loses its effectiveness as a bonding agent.

Organic Mastic The term for organic adhesives made from compounds of hydrocarbon molecules. They have either a latex or petroleum base and consist of two elements: a bonding agent and a binder.

Outside Corner A joint formed when two flat surfaces meet at an angle greater than 180 degrees.

Particleboard A man-made product made of a mixture of hard-setting resins and wood particles. Particle size determines whether the board will be designated as flakeboard (large particles) or chipboard (smaller particles). Particleboard is extruded into panels that range in thickness from $1/4$ to $1\,1/2$ inches and are available in dimensions of 4 × 8 feet. Panels are produced in three different densities and are graded with a number and letter. The number indicates the resin used in composition; the letter indicates the density.

Paver A tile produced mainly for floor use. They are usually made by the dust-pressed method and range in size from 6 to 12 inches square. They may be glazed or unglazed and can be up to $3/4$ inch thick. Machine-made pavers are fired at high temperatures, making them semivitreous. Manufactured pavers are usually sealed for protection from excessive wear and from staining. Handmade tiles are fired at lower temperatures and are nonvitreous. Also, they may not be sealed.

Penny (d) The symbol designating the size of nails. Derived from the English practice of selling 100 nails in English pence.

Perimeter Joint An expansion joint installed around the margin of a floor to absorb seasonal expansion.

Perimeter Tiles Tiles around the edge of the field.

Phosphoric Acid A mild acid used to clean discolored grout.

Pillowed Tiles Tiles that have a slightly convex or puffed up cross section.

Plumb A term used to designate a surface that is perfectly vertical.

Plumb Bob A pointed weight attached to a length of cord. The plumb is used to make sure that a surface is perfectly vertical or "plumb." The plumb bob is allowed to hang free so gravity can stretch the line and bring it to a vertical position.

Plywood Wood panels made of very thin layers of wood (called "plies," or "veneers") that are aligned at right angles and glued together. The opposing grain angles give the plywood more strength than solid wood. Panels range in thickness from $1/8$ to $3/4$ inch and are available in 4-foot-wide by 8-foot-long dimensions. Plywood is graded according to the number of blemishes on each side. Construction-grade plywood is manufactured for exterior and interior use and is designed to be covered with other surfacing materials.

Polymer-Modified Additive Latex or acrylic additive used to strengthen a mix of adhesive, grout, or mortar. The additive may be in dry form contained in the prepared mix, or it may be in liquid form to be added by the user.

Porcelain Tiles Dense, high-quality, vitreous tiles made by the dust-pressed method.

Porosity The capacity of unglazed tile to absorb water.

Primer A sealer applied to a substrate to prevent moisture or color from bleeding through to the top layers.

Quarry Tiles Natural clay vitreous tiles, at least $1/2$ inch thick, made by extrusion. Because of their density, they are a good choice for floor applications.

Reducing Strip Tiles Tiles with a raked profile and installed between two surfaces of dissimilar heights. The reducing strip effects a subtle transition between the two levels.

Reference Lines Two lines—one vertical, the other horizontal—that intersect at right angles to form the starting point for a tile installation.

Reinforcing Mesh Wire screening used to strengthen a mortar bed.

Retarder Additive An admixture added to adhesive to prolong the curing time.

Rubber Float (also called "grout flout") A float with a soft rubber face designed to apply grout.

Running Bond A common setting pattern for installing tiles. This pattern differs from a jack-on-jack pattern in that the grout lines are staggered much like the pattern in a brick wall. The tiles start on a horizontal course and are built up in successive courses.

Saltillo A tile produced in certain regions of Mexico. It is usually made of unprocessed clay.

Score To cut a shallow groove in tile or wallboard prior to cutting. The ends, on either side of the score line, are then bent back to snap the tile, or wallboard, into a break at the line.

Screed A straight-edged tool (usually a board) used to level a mortar bed by removing excess mud.

Sealer A transparent liquid applied to protect and waterproof tile or grout.

Semivitreous Tiles Tiles that have an absorption rate of from 3 to 7 percent of their weight. In terms of absorption, semivitreous tiles are between very porous nonvitreous tile and nonporous vitreous tile. With proper waterproofing, semivitreous tiles can be used for wet interior locations, but they are not freeze/thaw stable, so they are not a good choice for outdoor applications.

Setting-Bed The surface on which tiles are installed.

Setting Tiles The technique of placing the tiles in the adhesive to install them.

Set-Up Time The amount of time that an adhesive can be worked before it starts to cure.

Shims Thin wooden wedges inserted between framing members to adjust alignments, prevent movements, or correct sagging.

Skim Coat A thin coat of adhesive spread on a substrate to fill cracks and imperfections and to seal the surface prior to applying the final bonding coat.

Snap Cutter A hand-operated tool for cutting tiles. Strictly speaking, the snap cutter does not cut the tiles. Instead it breaks or snaps a tile along a scored line.

Spacers Small plastic pieces, manufactured in various shapes, that are inserted between tiles to establish and maintain uniform joint gaps.

Spackling Compound A white paste with a gypsum base used to cover nail heads and to paste tape on joints in wallboard.

Spading The technique of repeatedly inserting and withdrawing a shovel from a fresh mortar bed to break up and remove air pockets.

Striking Joints The technique of shaping grout or mortar joints.

Stub Walls Short partial walls that form the entrance to a shower.

Stud A vertical construction member that provides support and structure in a wall. Most studs are made of either wooden 2 X 4s or steel.

Stud Finder A magnetic or electronic tool used to locate wall studs.

Subfloor A rough floor covering laid down on the joists, to be later covered with finish flooring.

Substrate The backing on which tiles or other materials are installed.

Surround The tiled walls around a bathtub or shower area.

Tab-Mounted Tiles Sheet tiles held together with small circles of plastic or rubber.

Tamp To compact by repeatedly pressing or ramming.

T-Bolts Vertical bolts that hold a toilet to the floor.

TCA (Tile Council of America) An industry organization that studies and develops installation materials and methods, monitors product standards and quality, and promotes the use of American tiles to builders, architects, and do-it-yourselfers.

Terra-Cotta Tiles Tiles, sometimes glazed, made from fired raw earth. Used primarily for floor applications.

Tessera Small, hard-bodied tiles used for creating mosaics. *See also* Mosaic Tiles.

Thick-Bed Installation An installation that uses mortar for the setting bed.

Thinset Adhesive A powdered cement-based adhesive that must be mixed with liquid, water, latex, acrylic, or epoxy prior to use. Thinset adhesive has a greater bonding strength and is more water-resistant than organic mastic. It has become the standard for the tile-installation industry.

Thinset Installation Tile installation where the tile is set in adhesive that is less than $1/4$ inch thick.

Tile Cutter A tool for cutting tiles. A wet saw that has a rotating diamond wheel and a water spray is one example of a tile cutter. Another type of tile cutter is a handheld grinder fitted with an abrasive disk. Still another type of tile cutter is a snap cutter.

Tile Heritage Foundation A nonprofit organization dedicated to praising the value of old tile. The organization provides a list of noteworthy installations and sites and also provides an information network for building and architectural historians and interested persons. It has a library and research facility and sells tiles by mail order. In addition, the organization offers help to installers in need of specific tiles for restoration work.

Tile Nippers A plier-like tool used to grip and break off small pieces to make irregular-shaped cuts in a tile.

Toe-Space (also called a "kick space" or kick plate") A recessed area at the base of cabinets designed to accommodate feet.

Tongue-and-Groove Tiles Tiles that have grooves cut into some of the edges and projections and tongues cut into the others. The edges are then fitted together so the tongues mate into the grooves to create a strong joint.

TPB (Tile Promotion Board) An organization that provides consumer information and sources for domestic and imported tiles.

Trim Tiles Tiles with one or more finished edges. Trim tiles are used to finish the edges of a tile field.

Underlayment Panels of plywood, particleboard, or backer board used to create a support of substrate for a tile installation.

Uniform Building Code A building code published by the International Conference of Building Officials setting forth the structural requirements for most residential and commercial structures.

Utility Knife A knife with a short, sharp, replaceable blade used for general-purpose cutting and for scoring the face paper of wallboard to facilitate snapping it in two.

Vitreous Tiles Tiles that are fired at high temperatures for a long period of time. This produces dense-bodied tiles that absorb very little water, are stable during freeze/thaw cycles, and have high compression strength.

Wainscoting Wall treatment that only extends halfway, usually to chair height, up the wall.

Wallboard A structural board of any of various materials such as wood pulp, gypsum, or plastic made in large rigid sheets and used especially for sheathing interior walls and ceilings.

Water Absorption (also called "porosity") The capacity of tile to soak up water.

Waterproofing Membrane (also called "vapor barrier") A thin, flexible polyethylene film or building felt (about 4 mil thick) designed to prevent moisture from penetrating to the substrate.

Zellij Morrocan hand-cut tiles in traditional designs.

METRIC EQUIVALENTS CHART

INCHES TO MILLIMETERS AND CENTIMETERS
MM=Millimeters CM=Centimeters

Inches	MM	CM	Inches	MM	CM
1/8	3	0.3	$1^1/_2$	38	3.8
1/4	6	0.6	$1^3/_4$	44	4.4
3/8	10	1.0	2	51	5.1
1/2	13	1.3	$2^1/_2$	64	6.4
5/8	16	1.6	3	76	7.6
3/4	19	1.9	$3^1/_2$	89	8.9
7/8	22	2.2	4	102	10.2
1	25	2.5	$4^1/_2$	114	11.4
$1^1/_4$	32	3.2	5	127	12.7

INDEX